THE JAR SPELLS

COMPENDIUM

CHANGE YOUR LIFE AND
MANIFEST YOUR DESIRES.
100 EFFECTIVE BOTTLE
SPELLS RECIPES TO
ACHIEVE LOVE, HEALTH,
SUCCESS AND MORE

CRYSTAL BELL

Table of Contents

Introduction

Introduction

Essentially, a "magic spell" is a basic ritual that is performed in order to manifest an intention, to bring about a change to our life or situation. As such, spells can consist of any number of elements, in keeping with the Wiccan tradition of diversity, inclusivity, and its non-dogmatic approach. Understanding the core principles of Wicca will assist you in understanding the true power of spells—their ability to assist you in conducting the energy derived from the material and spiritual planes into creating positive results for your life.

Two rules dominate the Wiccan belief system, no matter what branch you attend or coven you belong to. The first is the Wiccan Rede, which is a kind of code of ethics that informs Wiccan behavior and attitudes: while the Rede itself is transliterated in different ways, it could be summed up as "that it harms none, do as thou wilt," a kind of paganized version of the Golden Rule. Basically, whatever you do, causes no harm to others; contrary to the Christian Golden Rule, it implicitly sanctions behavior that isn't necessarily mainstream or in keeping with Western religious traditions—as long as no harm comes to others (and one might add, to nature itself). The other main tenant of Wiccan belief is the Rule of Three: whatever energy you put out into the world, this rule says, it comes back to you three-fold. This is an incentive to live in harmony not just with your fellow humans but with nature and the environment, as well. Of course, this idea is not unique to Wiccan belief; it bears a striking resemblance to the Eastern notion of karma. Thus, any spells cast within a Wiccan framework will consciously follow these two tenants.

While Wicca claims its roots in a very long tradition of beliefs and fears regarding witches and witchcraft, its true origins are still yet fairly modern. Rooted in traditions of pre-Christian styles of pagan worship, Wicca was reborn in the mid-twentieth century as a religion of nature worship and a celebration of female power to equal the male. Many practitioners of Wicca can trace a direct line to pagan worship during pre-Christian Europe (such as Druidism), though many modern practices were inaugurated during the 1950s and refined during the 1980s by several influential figures and events. Additionally, many current believers also connect Wiccan belief and practice to Asian and Native American traditions, as well. Wicca is, at its core, an inclusive religion and set of beliefs that emphasize harmony with nature and a sense of spirituality that is not based on the Judeo-Christian, male-centered system of belief. Indeed, it is not anchored to any other system of belief; rather, it is a practice that takes its cues from some older (mostly pagan) practices and beliefs but relies on the individual to mold and shape those practices for their own positive intentions.

Concerning the power of spells, this means that you are attuning your energy to larger natural and spiritual forces, channeling this combination into a specific intention. This is usually done using a combination of tools—such as candles, crystals, runes, and other items—within a sacred or cleansed space.

Our various notions of how to perform "magic" or "cast spells" are generally derived from a host of stereotypes coming down to us from Hollywood movies and popular culture, in general (certainly, the Harry Potter juggernaut put spell-

3

making into everyone's vernacular these past twenty years). These images are harmless fun, but they belie the underlying power of the actual magic that emanates from nature and spirit. Wiccan magic—or, "magic," as it is often spelled—is much subtler and more powerful than any kind of wand-waving we may see portrayed in pop culture; learning to direct the energies of the universe toward creating positive change in your life is one of the most awesome magical tricks one can perform.

In general, most Wiccan magic is intended to engender positive change in the practitioner's life—most frequently in the arenas of love, wealth, and well-being (physically and emotionally). There are also spells of protection that are often cast, whether it be for home and hearth or against negative forces and possibilities. Thus, spells for a romantic connection, professional success, safe travel, and a quick recovery from illness or bad luck are popular. Not all magic is performed solely for the benefit of the practitioner, however—many spells are cast for the well-being of others, either people that the Wicca may know or for humankind as a whole. Some covens regularly practice spells that are designed to promote healing after a natural disaster, for example, or to encourage the healing and resilience of the earth under threat from climate change. One of the overall goals of Wiccan practice is to bolster spiritual growth and connection, in general, so the kinds of spells one casts are in keeping with this broader view.

Casting spells is only one form of magic, and all forms of magic are in some sense casting a spell (enchantment, incantation, and charms are all derivative of the same Latin phrasing meaning "to sing" with its attendant magical associations). So, aside from incantations and charms, a Wicca might also practice divination—looking to the future to see a clearer pathway—or create potions. Both of these things are often done in combination with

4

incantations—the casting of spells. A variety of these methods will be explored throughout this, divided into segments based on the overall intention of the magic and/or spell.

In particular, much of Wiccan magic is highly ritualized; that is, it is inspired by the magic of ceremonial tradition that is derived from the long history of magic in European cultures, specifically, with some Asian influence. Thus, we will also be exploring how to set up an altar, use symbols and tools, and other elements of ritual practice. All Wiccans utilize natural elements within their practice and spell-casting, such as candles, crystals and stones, herbs, plants, shells, and so on. This is paying homage to the very natural world that grants us this energy and this ability to direct these universal connections toward our particular intentions. A Wiccan is also familiar with the power of the four basic elements—earth, air, water, and fire—and how they connect to either the Mother Goddess (the feminine forces of the universe, represented by earth and water) or to the Horned God (the masculine forces of the universe, represented by air and fire). These forces work in opposition and balance at the same time, and the most powerful Wiccans understand how to channel these various energies in their best spell-casting. These elements also correspond to the four cardinal directions: the earth is oriented toward the north; air to the south; water to the west; and fire to the east. This orientation assists the practitioner in how to set up ritual space, as well as how to direct particular energies for specific purposes.

Also, to take into consideration are the phases of the moon and the patterns of the seasons. The Wheel of the Year—the Wiccan calendar—indicates the passing of the seasons in a very specific and natural manner, showcasing the equinoxes and solstices alongside the quarter segments of the year to determine the most auspicious times for certain celebrations and rituals. The Sabbats—

5

Wiccan holidays—are organized according to this calendar. Various symbols represent myriad ideas within the realm of Wiccan belief, the pentacle is one of the most powerful; these symbols can be used to evoke certain powers or energies within spell-casting and ritual practice in general.

Spell Jars: What Exactly Are They?

Sometimes also called *bottled spells or witch's jars*, these small glass bottles sealed with candle wax and capped with a cork or lid represent a magical tool used for protection, break a curse, or repel bad energies and magical attacks.

As indicated, in ancient times, they were usually filled with things like old rusty nails, razor blades, shards of glass, urine, and other objects with specific qualities and great magical potency, known in the Craft as catalysts.

They used to be buried or hidden near the maker's home to absorb the evil forces that had been sent to them. This is why a few centuries ago, it was completely normal for a family to have a bottle buried on their property for abundance and protection.

People who feared to be already cursed might also choose to throw their jar into the fire, knowing that when the bottle exploded, it meant the spell had been broken. In other words, these charms were used as a form of protection or "counter magic," a means of blocking and trapping the harmful effects of witchcraft in different folk traditions.

But spell jars could also be used to make curses, not only to protect from them. In that case, part of the victim's (not maker's) urine, hair, or nail clippings, was placed in the bottle along with threads to simulate "traps." Other commonly used ingredients were seawater, dirt, sand, stones, knotted ropes, feathers, shells, herbs, flowers, salt, oil, or ashes. And again, also rusty nails, thorns, pieces of glass, wood, and bone.

Modern witches have begun using bottles for spells with the function of protection rather than making a curse.

This is why, nowadays, a spell jar is considered to be a tool specially prepared to stop any negativity.

Overall, it is used as a protective element of the home as its presence cancels evil spells, stops psychic attacks, annuls enemy conspiracies, unfair competition, hatred, friends with double standards, or mean family members.

It is also recommended to ward off misfortune, accidents, falls, or illnesses. In other words, it works as an absorbent sponge of negative energies, collecting any possible toxic element.

Overall, the most popular witch bottles are those intended for protection due to their high effectiveness. But at the same time, spell jars are also prepared to attract love, money, prosperity, etc.

Generally, modern witches put specific ingredients into the jar to match their intention. For example, a witch that wants to attract love will fill her bottle with things like red wine, lavender buds, apple slices, and rose quartz. Then, after consecrating the bottle with a spell, she may leave it in her bedroom to attract the lover of her dreams. Similarly, a bottle can also be placed in the room of someone sick to absorb their illness. Later, its contents are thrown out and buried to disperse it.

As indicated, according to tradition, once made, the bottle should be buried in the house's garden. However, nowadays, many people choose to hide it somewhere safe at home, place it in their bag or pour its contents into a river or sea to flow, just to name a few examples.

Overall, no matter if you wish to attract wealth, happiness, friendship, work, health, protection, intuition, or love... there are as many types of bottles as people who make them.

And by using plants and elements appropriate for the purpose you are specifically looking for; you can create a very effective tool to accomplish all your dreams.

I have provided you with a wide array of spells with varied purposes and uses. With a positive attitude, you can use these to fulfill your wishes. I hope you find what you are looking for in this book and wish you happy spell casting!

Chapter 1. Fundamentals of Jar Spells and the Concept of Intent

Instructions for Spell Casting

A spell refers to a magical formulation that is normally intended to trigger a magic effect on either a person or an object. The spells are normally created through the chanting of a series of words, singing, or even mere speaking. The series of words are known to have magical powers, and a person or object under a particular spell has their actions and thoughts dictated by the specification of said spell. Usually, the spells are cast by witches or groups of persons who believe in their powers, and they are believed to cause instantaneous reactions.

Creating your own Wiccan spells is actually simpler than believed to be. While most witches and spell casters usually use ancient spells created by other people, there are times when they want to use customized and specific spells. In this case, the writing of individual spells is imminent.

It all depends on your preference, if you want to perform spells or not, either way, it is not compulsory to do spells and magic to be Wiccan. Further, if you want to create or do spells, remember the creed "Harm None" as this is an essential part of Wicca. It doesn't mean that if you perform spells, you can destroy your enemies this is NOT true! If this is your motive for becoming a Wicca, then I suggest you stop reading this book as it won't get you near your goal. So, I repeat, the practice of Wicca is to commune with nature and to open the realm of the gods and goddesses to be one with them through connecting with nature.

When it comes to witch craft, making a spell is easy it's just like creating a new home-cooked meal recipe; but of course, it requires practice. So, let's just stick to how spells are generally done.

Your Purpose

The first step in doing a spell is to know what the purpose of the spell is. The goal has to be specific. For example, if you are looking for love, a love spell won't do the trick because are you already eyeing someone? Or maybe you want an ex to come back to you? Or maybe you still need to meet that special someone. This is how specific your purpose should be.

Materials

The next step is finding the 'perfect' spell and gathering all the necessary materials to do the spell. You can also make your spell by making use of 'correspondences' as these are lists of items with their corresponding purposes. Take for example you can use the herb Damiana which corresponds to lust and love. To make a spell, would need around 2 to 5 items are sufficient. You can also make use of crystals or candles and work with colors too.

Words

When casting a spell, using words best helps you to focus your intention and energy. Some spells already have words included. But if you are making your own spell, then you have to be creative when it comes to creating chants.

Timing

Although this is not as important as other steps in casting a spell, with the right timing, it can add additional power to your spell. For a little magical boost, you can pick the right phase of the moon or the right day of the week. Check out some correspondence tables to boost the power of your spell.

Put It All Together

Many people believe that just chanting the words of a spell and going through the motions will lead to a successful spell. But in reality, what makes a good spell powerful and successful depends on your focus. You have to focus on what you are doing and you have to take your time. Thus, it means you need to learn the spell before you begin. You also need to visualize the energy and your intentions as vividly as you can and this is the hardest part when casting spells because it takes practice and experience.

How to Create Your Own Wiccan Spells Following the Aforementioned Instructions

The following represents a simple formula to create your own spells:

Identification of the Key Intent/Goal of the Spell

Before you get down to the writing of a spell, you must begin by establishing the key intent/end goal. Each spell works to achieve a particular purpose, and you must be able to identify exactly what you want to achieve. People cast spells for different purposes. These purposes can include the desire to find love, success, employment, or good health. Through the creation of the spell, the major goal is attracting exactly what you want to have in your life. Whatever the main aim is, make sure to attain specificity. Examples of intentional aims include the following:

- I will get the advertised job.
- I will be promoted to the next level.
- I will find my soul mate.
- I will heal from arthritis.

In some instances, you may want to write a spell that is directed to another person. It may be that you would like a good fortune for the other party or you would like to punish them for something. Whatever your aim is, you must keep in mind that karma is real and that what you cast upon others can come back to you at any time. It is for this reason that one of the basic tenets of Wicca practice is the stipulation that you must take care that your activities do not bring harm to others.

Determining and Assembling the Materials Needed

In the course of casting a spell, various materials are required for specific spells. You must determine what materials you need to use to be successful in the casting of your spells. According to Wicca, the greater magic often lies in the symbols, which makes it imperative to learn some of the basics symbols that pertain to your spell and use them. Notably, the fact that the Wicca tradition is ancient does not mean that the use of current items is out of bounds. The wheels of cars, sunglasses and even chess boards can be used as long as you are clear about what they are meant to symbolize.

In determining the materials, you will use, you must always keep in mind that spells serve two key purposes: to either attract something into your life or banish something. The former is usually positive while the latter serves as a protection against aspects such as illnesses and spells cast by other people. The materials used to achieve the two are very different, hence the need for clarity. Currently, there are very many books and publications that help you choose the materials and ingredients; it is ideal that you decide upon those that most appeal to you.

Decide on the Timing

As has been stated, most of the spells are very time-specific, although there are a few that are not. In most cases, the timing of the spells is highly dependent on the phases of the moon, as some spells are cast during the full moon and others are cast in alternate moon iterations. In most cases, spells that are supposed to bring positivity and beneficial inferences to you are conducted during the full moon or when the waxing moon appears. Destruction spells or generally negative spells that are required to banish some of the retrogressive

14

aspects of your life are conducted during the waning phase. In as much as the specific details are really not as important as they seem, it is worth understanding that the energies during the particular phases are different, which makes it imperative to ensure that you follow the periods as much as you possibly can. It's worth noting that you can write your own Book of Shadows based on your individual experiences when casting spells, and the greatest aspect that you must observe is to be immensely confident about what you are doing.

Figure Out the Words

For spells to work, specific incantations and chants must be used. As the Wiccan say, there is power in words. There are no words that are chanted in the spell making that are void. Currently, anyone can have access to the hundreds of Wiccan spells that are found both online and in publications, and you can identify the specific one that you wish to use. Some spells are meant to call the gods for assistance while other spells are used in poetic inferences. However, all work the same, and the only thing you need to do is make sure that by making the chants, you will invoke the particular occurrence that you desire.

Setting Up Your Altar

An Altar is a space of devotion to something. We all need a place in our homes that reflects our most important desires and passions as well as our thoughts and expectations. An altar is a perfect way to create a physical manifestation of your spiritual journey.

There are no rules to setting up your altar and sometimes, it will change with you as you grow and evolve. It takes on the life you are living as you add and subtract things from it based on the intentions and practices you are doing.

Altars are a reflection of who you are and what you are praying to and so while you develop your own altar, be clear about how it shows off what you are choosing to align with at all times. It needs to be a place that has a flow and energy of harmony and balance. It may be necessary for you to tend to your altar daily or frequently to maintain its energy and ability to attract abundance into your life.

Your altar should be in a place in your home where it cannot be disturbed easily by others and can be easily seen by you so that you are always alive to it. Many people put altars where anyone can see them and that is perfectly okay; it doesn't need to be hidden; it only needs space to exist undisturbed by anyone but you.

The altar of your choice can be on a bookshelf, in a cabinet, on top of your dresser, hanging on the wall, *etc.*

Many times, people will use a cloth to lay out on the surface of wherever it will sit. It could be something small, like a scarf or a handkerchief or it could be something more meaningful, like a piece of heirloom lace from your grandmother. You don't have to use cloth at all, but if you choose to, make sure it is something that reflects the overall energy of your altar.

Next, you can start bringing in objects to help you align with your spiritual path and purpose. Many people place sculptures or figurines of their favored gods and goddesses, others may use paintings, pictures, or photographs to set out as an homage to a particular deity. Anything goes really and it all depends on what you like and what you are wanting to focus on.

Another approach is to just use the items from your tool kit. You can place these items on the altar and dedicate this space to your sacred rituals so that your tools are always resting on your altar. Essentially, building an altar for your magical tools. Bringing focus to these items through the display on an altar will remind you of the importance of working with this magic and will help you continue to honor your Wiccan practice. When you are opening your energies to work with your tools, you can start by lighting candles on your altar, burning some incense, or smudging the altar and starting your rituals in this way.

Your altar is a display of your internal magical self. It is a reflection of your power and your curiosity to ask questions about the great unknown and to worship the energy of all things in this world. Bring to your altar anything that is resonating with you at the time. You may decide to decorate it with fresh-cut flowers and let them wilt and dry to illustrate the idea of life and death.

You may also want to collect items from your nature walks to devote the altar to Mother Earth. It can also be a place that changes with every Wiccan holiday celebration making your altar devotion to the seasons and rhythms of the Earth.

Don't be afraid to alter your altar. It can transform with you as you grow and it will need to be tended to the way you tend to yourself. Treat it like a living thing and as an expression of yourself. Whatever water you keep on your altar, if any, needs to be clean and pure; don't let it get dirty and stagnant as that will be a sign showing you that you are neglecting your altar and your spiritual practice.

Tend to it and allow it to be a consistently transforming part of your life that invokes a deeper spiritual reflection of your journey.

Asking the Gods/Goddesses for Support

Whether you are looking for guidance from the gods and goddesses of Pagan ritual or not, letting yourself be open to their assistance and guidance is a good way to bond with the energies of all things as you work with your Wiccan practices. You may not have a particular deity that you work with or devote your altar to but as you are preparing your rituals, it is a good idea to let the universal energies know that you are ready to tap in and find help if it is offered as you cast your spells and perform your rituals.

All you have to do is say the following words as you light the candles on your altar and burn your incense:

"I am opening the lights of all life to the energy of all things. I ask for guidance, support, and protection from the Great Mother and Father and all offerings from the spirits and deities of all life. I am open to receive your love, light, and warmth as I progress in my ritual. So, mote it be."

You can change the wording to be anything that feels right for you based on what energies you want to call in to help. You may be more inclined to practice fairy magic or to work with the animal kingdom of spirit guides. You may also desire to connect with your ancestors as you begin your rituals and spell castings. All of these ways of connecting to that work will help you, so make sure it is in alignment with how your individual Wiccan practice is for you.

Change the wording of the above message to reflect your practice but keep the message the same. Stating that you are open to receive help and guidance is a very powerful tool of connection. Maintaining a desire to only work with the

18

energies of light and love is an important factor because it declares that you are wanting to work with the higher vibrations and that you don't want to call on anything harmful or low energy like a trickster spirit or energy who may not be as helpful as other energies will be.

Casting Your Circle

You don't have to use your altarpiece to cast your circle. You may be out in the woods when you need to cast and will be far away from your altar. It might be also that you just utilize your altar to store your magical tools between casting and won't need to involve it in your Wicca work; however, you may find that you feel more grounded in your practices if you start by connecting with the energy of your altar before casting your circle.

Why do you cast a circle and what does it even mean? When you are invoking the energies all around you and connecting your own energy to the spiritual plane, you need to have an opening and closing of intention and protection. It is a helpful way for you to have clarity and focus while you are performing rituals and casting spells but it also serves as an intentional centering of your energy and attachment to your spiritual self. Casting is almost like a meditation to get you engaged with your work.

The meaning of casting a circle in your preparation is also to align you with the four directions and the four elements. Each way you travel is represented by your circle and each element of the life spark is represented to connect you to your full purpose and potential. It is a meaningful acknowledgment of your journey when you cast a circle and it brings into focus that which helps you succeed on your path: the directions and the elements.

Spells, Rituals, Intentions

The next step in the process of a typical spell or ritual is the actual spell work or ritual work that aligns you with your intentions. Remember: it is important to have clear intentions before going in, so before you cast your circle, ask yourself: what is my magical purpose today?

Once you have clarity about what you are wanting to achieve or focus on, you may want to design your ritual or spell from your personal idea of how it should go or you can use already existing spells and craft work that feel natural and good for what you are wanting to accomplish. There are tons of spells online, in books, all over, that can help you choose the best way for you to align with your craft work.

Much of what you will be doing in this step is clearly detailing and stating your intentions to create the energy of life around it. It may include herbs and other items that support your intention. If you are celebrating a holiday or a specific god or goddess, you will be working with those items and energies specifically to enhance your ritual or spell.

Words are important and you may need to write down ahead of time the words you want to share once you have opened a circle. Preparing for your ritual or spell is just as important as executing it. Before opening your circle, write down the words for your spell on a piece of paper. Gather the herbs you wish to include in your circle or the relics and objects that will be meaningful to you.

There are so many unique possibilities for how you can invoke your own powerful magic and let it be known to the energies of all that surrounds you. The following steps are simple ideas and clues for how you can get started with creating your ritual and spell. Remember that practicing Wicca is a creative and artistic experience and there really isn't a wrong way to do it.

Set your intention. Write it on paper, on leaves, on stones or pieces of wood to burn, on anything magical. Gather your ingredients. You may be working with herbal remedies that support your intention. Make a bouquet of them to dry on your altar. Collect the stones, crystals, and any other earth elements that feel appropriate and place them where they feel best. You may want to collect sacred water from a waterfall or a river that feels magical to you. After casting your circle of protection and power, you can now begin your ritual with your objects and intentions. Using your written intentions as a declaration is a wonderful way to open yourself up to the energy of what you are wanting to accomplish. Don't just write it on the paper or the leaves; read it aloud so that you can feel the words come out of your mouth with a sound and release the words into your circle.

Closing Your Circle

Closing your circle is as simple as opening it. All you have to do is pay respect and gratitude to the elements and the directions. You may want to face each direction again to ask the directions to comfort you on your path as you allow your spell to take effect.

You can also connect with the elements you have in your space and carefully return them to their altar space as a way of creating closure with them. Here are a few steps to help you close your circle, as you opened it:

Thank each element by addressing it directly. Example: Thank you to the earth that grounds me (sprinkle salt or soil into your hands and rub them together, letting the salt/soil fall away naturally). Thank you to the air that blows me forward on my journey (snuff out the smudge stick). Thank you to the fire the lights my way (blow out the candle). Thank you to the water that cleanses and purifies (dip fingers in water and flick on your altar or your own face). Stand up or point your energy in the direction of each of the four directions to thank them for their presence, similar to the way you did it with the elements in Step 1. All you have to do is offer gratitude and move through each direction, closing the circle the way it started.

Alternative: You can combine steps 1 and 2 and close the circle by thanking each direction and the corresponding element simultaneously.

A final thank you can be expressed to the Great Mother and the Father or whichever gods/goddesses you have invoked for your ritual.

Casting spells requires a lot of confidence and belief that whatever you are invoking will come to pass. You must not have any doubt in your mind or heart, as this may hinder the full connection with the energies and the gods. Notably, casting spells using your own words and chants is considered to be more effective than using other people's spells. Whenever you use your own spell and words, the energy connection is much greater than the use of other people's creativity. Personal spells create your signature and a unique energy connection; you just need to have total belief.

Accepting Your True Power

Wicca is a beautiful, fun and magical way to connect with your true power and the energy of all life around you. It has a way of asking you to be present and to identify your whole being and the nature of what you are seeking with a mindful appreciation of nature and all of your energies.

One of the most profound lessons of Wicca and other Pagan practices is that it is a way for you to creatively explore yourself and your inner power as you transform and grow. The best way for you to approach rituals and casting spells is to trust your inner knowing about how the spell should go and what ways it can unfold.

You will find a wide range of variations for one specific intention or spell because there isn't a wrong way to cast. As long as you are upholding the Wiccan Rede, then anything goes, essentially. As you continue to work with your own spell work and rituals, remember to honor your power above all else. Devotions to the Earth Mother and all of the other gods and goddesses are equally important to the devotion of your own magical powers and truths.

Magickal Ethics

Harm None

Not every spellcaster will be a follower of Wicca. But this section is included because it is a good way for you to learn about the severe consequences of your actions when you're in the caster's position.

This is the most essential rule for all magickal workings. This means that you should only use magick to benefit yourself or others. Do not use magick to harm someone else.

In addition, two additional rules are commonly used when casting spells:

1. As above, so below.

2. What goes around comes around.

Let's look at each of these rules in more detail.

Rule 1 – As Ye Harm None, Do as Ye Will

This is the first rule of Wicca. It states that you should only cast magick for good purposes. There are no exceptions to this rule.

It is straightforward to fall into thinking that magick works differently than ordinary life. We often think that magick is like magic tricks where we pull rabbits out of hats. However, this is not true. Magick is natural, powerful, and dangerous.

When you use magick, you are making changes in reality. These changes may seem small at times, but they can significantly impact our lives.

For example, if you cast a spell to make your ex-girlfriend jealous, she will start acting crazy toward you. She might even try to break up with you. You may think this is just an illusion, but it isn't. It is really happening.

When you cast a spell, you send out thought waves of energy. These thoughts create vibrations in the ether. The vibrations then attract similar vibrations from other people. This results in the creation of what is called a magnetic field.

The magnetic field attracts matter (like air molecules). Once the issue is attracted, it starts vibrating. This vibration creates a wave pattern that travels through space. This is why you can feel the effects of magick.

Rule 2 - What Goes Around Comes Around

This is another important rule of Wicca and magick. Essentially, it says that everything returns to its original state. That means that whatever you send out, you will eventually get back.

For example, let's say you cast a spell to bring you some extra cash. You believe that this will help you pay off your debts. After a few days, you get a raise at work. Then, after a few months, you find out that you have been promoted.

Basically, this is what happened. Your spell worked perfectly! Now, you owe less money, and you have more money. What went around came around!

Is Wicca Practiced by All Witches?

No. Today, witches all over the world are believers in mainstream religions. Many of them believe in God and follow Christian values. Some are Jewish, Hindu, Mormon, Baha'i, Muslim, Buddhist, Taoist, etc., but they still believe that witchcraft is real.

In fact, many people have a misconception about what witchcraft really means. They think it's just some kind of black magic or voodoo. But this isn't true because there is no such thing as witchcraft without religion. You can't practice witchcraft if you don't believe in supernatural power.

Witchcraft has been around for centuries. It was practiced by ancient Egyptians, Greeks, Romans, Celts, Norsemen, Druids, Aztecs, Incas, Mayans, Hindus, Buddhists, Jews, Christians, Muslims, and others. Today, it's widely accepted as an alternative belief system.

Many people who practice witchcraft today say that they do so out of religious beliefs. Still, others see it as a way to connect with nature and learn more about spirituality. Most modern-day Witches are spiritual seekers who want to find answers to life's questions.

Is It Okay to Cast a Spell on Someone Who Doesn't Know About It?

Doing spells for others is something that has been around since ancient times. Spells were used to bring good luck or bad luck to people. Use of spells was also used as a form of punishment. People would cast spells on their enemies to cause harm. However, specific rules should always be followed when casting spells. These rules include knowing how to cast a spell correctly and knowing its purpose before releasing it.

In modern times, spells are still used but for different purposes. For example, some spells are used to bring good luck to people. This includes love spells, money spells, job spells, and even career spells. Other spells are used to punish people who have committed crimes against others. This includes revenge spells, curse removal spells, and even death spells.

When casting spells, certain precautions should be taken:

- First, you should ensure that the person who is being targeted knows about the spell.
- Second, you should only cast a spell if you are sure that the purpose of the spell will be fulfilled.
- Third, you should perform rituals to cleanse yourself before performing any spell.

- Fourth, you should never cast a spell without asking permission first.
- Fifth, you should never cast spells just for fun.
- Sixth, you should always follow the law when casting spells.

Finally, you should always be careful when casting spells because they can be dangerous. There can be dire consequences for dabbling in people's lives. If you always remember to try to practice all your craft with pure intentions, you can avoid disaster.

Magic Ethics for Spellcasters

Many people think that magic is just a game or something that only exists in movies, but there are real spells and rituals. There are also several ways people use their powers for good purposes, like healing others and helping people with their problems. But unfortunately, people also use some terrible practices when they cast spells. Here are some of the most common ones:

- **Using Spells to Get Attention**

One of the worst things you can ever do is use magic to get attention. This is because it is a very selfish thing to do. People usually use spells to get attention because they want to impress someone or even themselves. They may even use magic to get back at someone who has hurt them in the past. Therefore, using spells to get attention is not ethical.

- **Dabbling in Magick**

Dabblers are a dime a dozen, and they're dangerous. If you dabble in magick, you don't know what you're doing. As a result, you may end up hurting yourself or someone else. The best way to avoid this is by learning your craft and treating your spiritual journey like a lifelong relationship.

You will make mistakes. Just make sure you learn from them!

- **Not Knowing How Your Craft Works**

The other big problem with dabblers is that they don't really understand how their craft works. They don't know the difference between good and evil spells. They aren't aware of the differences between various types of magick. So, they disregard the threat of a spell backfiring.

- **Using Spells to Hurt Others**

Finally, another thing that you should never use your powers for is hurting others. Using your magick to intentionally harm others is just a rotten thing, but it is also dangerous for both you and your friends and family. Spells and curses often backfire and come back on the caster or spell buyer tenfold.

- **Acceptance of All Practitioners**

There are many different types of people who practice the craft and cast spells. Not all of them would identify with being called a witch or believed in Paganism or Wicca. Most witches would fall under the category of a solitary witch with a shot of eclectic witch and a splash of kitchen witch!

Sometimes the terms witchcraft and sorcery are used interchangeably, but they refer to different types of magical practice. For example, mysticism refers to using black magic, while witchcraft refers to white magic.

The term "witch" has been applied to many people throughout history, including shamans, priests, magicians, healers, mystics, prophets, seers, and fortune-tellers.

Many religions have elements of both white and black magic. The Universe always demands balance.

We've learned many things about magickal ethics. We've discussed the differences between ethical magick and unethical magick and the difference between moral magick and immoral magick. Magick is something that everyone does, whether they realize it or not. It's something that everyone uses every day, but rarely do people stop to examine their personal use of magick. By reviewing one's actions, magick users can better use magick for good.

Correspondences of Commonly Found Components

I have assembled this list of popular correspondences of commonly found components for quick reference. This appendix does not absolve you of the responsibility for developing your own sets of correspondences! No book can dictate how you use a substance's energies. These are guidelines only.

Colors

Red: life, passion, action, energy

Pink: affection, friendship

Orange: success, speed, career, action

Yellow: intellectual matters, communication

Light green: healing, wishes

Dark green: prosperity, money, nature

Light blue: truth, spirituality, tranquility, peace

Dark blue: healing, justice

Violet: mysticism, meditation, spirituality

Purple: occult power, spirituality

Black: protection, fertility, mystery

Brown: stability, home, career

White: purity, psychic development

Grey: calm, spirit work, gentle closure, neutralizing energy or situations

Silver: purity, divination, psychic work, feminine energy, spirit, lunar energy

Gold: health, prosperity, solar energy, masculine energy

Deities

I caution you against simply inserting the name and energy of a deity into your spell craft. Take the time to research the culture from which they derive. Look into the methods of spell craft and worship to which they are accustomed. You need to ascertain the correct and respectful approach to determine if it is indeed appropriate to work with them.

Most deities have name variations, as well as cultural and/or regional variations; I have not included all of this information simply because to do so would create another book in its own right. This is not by any means an exhaustive list; these are deities commonly found in myth and spell work.

Amaterasu (Japanese): the sun, ancestor of humanity, the seasons

Anubis (Egyptian): the underworld, otherworld guide, protection

Aphrodite (Greek): love, romance, sex, passion, women, lust, beauty

Apollo (Greek): the sun, arts, light, prophecy, logic, knowledge

Aradia (Italian): spell craft, magic

Arianrhod (Welsh): magic, female independence, virginity, the moon

Artemis (Greek): celibacy, fertility, hunting, protector of animals, the moon, birth, bees, bears

Athena (Greek): wisdom, the arts, crafts, negotiation, olives, virginity, community, owls, serpents, protection

Bast (Egyptian): love, the arts, luxury, cats, lioness, pleasure, dancing, music, joy, health

Brighid (Pan-Celtic): inspiration, creativity, animals, children, women, hearth and home, healing, smithcraft, metalwork, defense, fire, water, cattle, milk

Cernunnos (Pan-Celtic): forests, sovereignty, wildlife

Cerridwen (Welsh): inspiration, transformation, initiation, death and rebirth, wisdom

Danu (Irish): sovereignty, fertility

Demeter (Greek): the earth, agriculture, crops, motherhood

Diana (Roman): light, fertility, childbirth, the moon, hunting

31

Epona (Gaulish): horses, fertility, sovereignty

Eros (Greek): romance, passion, lust, physical love

Freyja (Norse): love, passion, death, shapeshifting, prophecy, fertility, lust, battle, falcons

Frigga (Norse): domestic balance, prophecy, herons

Ganesha (Hindu): wisdom, luck, study, prosperity, abundance

Gwydion (Welsh): spell craft, shapeshifting

Hecate (Greco-Roman): mysteries, the underworld, spell craft, spellcasters, justice, dogs, horses, serpents, the moon, wisdom

Hera (Greek): marriage, women, cuckoos, the three phases of womanhood: maiden, mother, and crone

Hermes (Greek): intellect, communication, commerce, messages, travel

Herne (British): hunting, forests, wild animals

Hestia (Greek): domestic balance, hearth, home, fire, community, family, hospitality

Horus the Elder (Egyptian): falcons, balance, solar and lunar energy, healing, the moon, the sun

Horus the Younger (Egyptian): humanity, rulership

Hygeia (Greek): healing, health

Inanna (Sumerian): fertility, sky, love

Isis (Egyptian): magic, women, the moon, culture, healing

Jupiter (Roman): business, career, leadership

Kuan Yin (Chinese): compassion, peace, mercy, rainbow, willow, generosity

Lakshmi (Hindu): wealth, abundance, cows, lotus, jewels

Lugh (Pan-Celtic): success, excellence, competition, adoption

Ma'at (Egyptian): justice, order, truth

Mercury (Roman): communication, commerce, travel, theft

Odhinn (Norse): wisdom, ravens, wolves, travel, poetry, sacrifice, mysteries

Osiris (Egyptian): resurrection, agriculture, the underworld, afterlife

Pan (Greek): lust, nature, wilderness, passion

Poseidon (Greek): sea, horses, dolphins

Rhiannon (Welsh): underworld, birds, journeying to the otherworld, horses, joy

Sarasvati (Hindu): water, eloquence, study, arts and sciences, writing, music, speech, genius, inspiration

Sulis (British): healing, water

Thor (Norse): weather, agriculture, working-class, soldiers, thunder, sky, farmers, sailors

Thoth (Egyptian): wisdom, time, architecture, language, mathematics, the moon, science

Tyr (Norse): law, justice, leadership

Candles

Many different types of candles are specific for effects and functions, and each one has been assigned to a specific spell. Some types might include seven-day candles, zodiac candles, pillars, and shapes. Pillar candles are the most common and can be used daily. They come in various colors and are used because of their longevity. Each candle has a specific use. Chakra candles get used to cleanse our bodies and to provide holistic effects. The shaped ones are used to cast specific spells.

- **Pillar, Jumbo, and Altar**

These candles are tall and thick. They burn slowly. This is why they are great to be used as deity or altar candles because they get lit first but extinguished last. These can also be found in glass containers such as seven-day candles.

- **Scented Candles**

You can use scented candles in your spells. Below you will find a chart that shows you the magical properties of every scent:

- Vanilla: enhance memory, sexual passion
- Tangerine: prosperity
- Strawberry: luck, friendship, love
- Sandalwood: purification, healing, protection
- Rose: love
- Pine: getting rid of negative energies, strength
- Patchouli: attracts money
- Myrrh: purification, protection
- Musk: courage, strength, sexual passion, love
- Lotus: inner peace, harmony

- Jasmine: love
- Honeysuckle: psychic abilities, healing, good luck
- Frangipani: attracts positive energy
- Coconut: protection, purification
- Cinnamon: good fortune, attracts wealth
- Cherry: attracts love
- Carnation: healing
- Blueberry: keeps negative energy away

- **Crucifix or Cross**

These candles can be used to banish spells or for protection. They are also very beneficial to be used as an offering to Lwa, a saint, God, deity, or Orisha.

- **Devil-Be-Gone and Satan**

These are in the shape of the Christian's devil and can be used to remove spirits, negative energies, entities, and exorcisms. Burn it with an astral candle to represent someone who needs to be cleansed.

- **Seven-Knob**

These candles consist of seven evenly sized knobs. Burn one each day while you are focusing on your desires, goals, and wishes. Because it takes seven days to completely burn, it makes your magic extremely potent. The following will help you know what color to burn:

- Blue: confusion, fights, stop depression
- Purple: spiritual protection and defeating spiritual attacks
- White: granting secret wishes, purification
- Yellow: removing bad luck

- Brown: justice spells
- Orange: getting rid of obstacles and business success
- Green: manifesting, court case spells, money spells
- Red: putting energy in motion, getting rid of obstacles, love spells
- Black: releasing spells, banishing spells

• **Skull and Mummy**

Skull candles look like skulls, and mummy candles look like a mummy lying in a coffin. These candles offer protection and are great when warding off death, illness, and dangerous situations.

• **Cat**

These will be in the shape of a cat, obviously. Use a black one to break jinxes, hexes, and to break curses. They can be used to attract good luck and to get rid of bad luck. A green one can help with healing and prosperity, especially if you are trying to heal your pet. If you want to increase the potency of love spells, use a red one.

• **Eve and Adam**

These are in the shape of a nude female and male. You can find them in many colors. They are used in attraction and love spells. You can use them to bring love to your life, bring back lost love, push away unwanted love, or break up relationships.

- **Zodiac or Astral**

These candles can represent another person or yourself in a ritual or spell. They have many uses and could be used in various rituals. Be sure that you never throw them away. You need to always allow them to burn out completely or store them safely. Use the color chart below to help you with your spells:

- o   Pisces: blue, green, white
- o   Aquarius: green, blue
- o   Capricorn: black, brown, red
- o   Sagittarius: purple, blue, red, gold
- o   Scorpio: red, black, brown
- o   Libra: light brown, blue, black
- o   Virgo: yellow, grey, black, gold
- o   Leo: orange, gold, green, red
- o   Cancer: white, brown, green
- o   Gemini: silver, yellow, blue, red
- o   Taurus: pink, green, yellow, red
- o   Aries: red, pink, white

- **Taper**

These candles are thin and tall, and you have to be careful when dressing and anointing them. These are best when quick results are needed. Make sure you always use a holder and be sure the ones you get are colored all the way through and not just on the outside.

- **Table**

These candles can be found in most stores and can be used in most rituals. Try to find the best quality and be sure they have not been dipped.

Stones

Agate: strength, courage, healing, protection

Agate, blue lace: peace, soothes stress, spirituality, inspiration, tranquility

Agate, moss: healing, strength, the plant world, agriculture

Amber: energy, healing, creativity, life, beauty, love, attraction

Amethyst: truth, protection, peaceful sleep, spirituality, soothes stress, courage, travel, meditation, psychic awareness, justice, beauty

Aquamarine: peace, joy, happiness, psychic powers

Aventurine: luck, fortune, money, mental powers, healing

Bloodstone (also known as "heliotrope"): healing, money, courage, strength, fertility

Carnelian: career, success, hunting, courage, confidence, ease nightmares

Citrine: eases nightmares, creativity, digestion

Fluorite: meditation, enhances energy, study, mental ability, amplifies other stones

Garnet: happiness, fidelity, strength, protection, healing

Hematite: grounding, protection from negative energy, healing

Howlite: communication, perception, intellectual pursuits, action

Jade: wealth, abundance, prosperity, money, business, love, friendship, healing, wisdom, protection

Jasper: energy, courage, strength, protection

Lapis lazuli: healing, wisdom, mental powers, joy, stress reliever, spirituality, peace, fidelity, psychic awareness, protection

Malachite: fertility, protection, travel, love, soothe stress, sleep, money

Moonstone: love, compassion, friendship, psychic powers, sleep

Obsidian: protection, divination, grounding

Onyx: protection

Pearl: lunar energy, water, love, luck

Rhodochrosite: energy, peace, love

Quartz, clear: energy, meditation, healing, psychic abilities

Quartz rose: peace, love, affection, beauty, children, comfort, fidelity

Sodalite: soothes stress, wisdom, emotional balance, meditation, peace

Tiger's eye: luck, wealth, honesty, protection, courage, confidence

Turquoise: eloquence, health, happiness, protects children, travel, money, beauty, luck

Metals

Aluminum: mental abilities, travel.

Brass: solar energy, healing, protection, money. An alloy of copper and zinc (communication, prosperity), brass can be used as a magical substitute for gold.

Copper: Venus, love, attraction, feminine energy, conducting energy, luck, energy, healing, money.

Gold: solar energy, purity, wealth, prosperity, success, energy. Also known for healing, protection, wisdom, and male fertility.

Iron: Mars, defense, protection from evil fairies and spirits, power, strength, grounding.

Lead: Saturn, the underworld, protection, defensive spells, divination, strength, community, leadership.

Mercury: Mercury, communication, links, mental agility. Also known as "quicksilver," mercury has been declared toxic and is very rarely found. In the past, it was used in thermometers. I have included the information here for the sake of reference.

Pewter: Alloy of mostly tin; has a small amount of antimony (advancement, determination, success) and traces of copper.

Platinum: harmony, health, relaxation.

Silver: lunar energy, the Goddess, purity, love, psychic abilities. Also known for peace, protection, money, and travel.

Steel: protection, healing, defense against nightmares. Steel is an alloy of iron with small amounts of carbon.

Tin: Jupiter, divination, luck, intellectual pursuits, new beginnings.

Herbs, Trees and Plants

Note: *Poisonous herbs are included in this list of correspondences and are labeled as "toxic."* I do not recommend using them, especially since there are several other components with a similar energy that can be used instead. However, you may run across references to them in other spell books, so I have listed them here.

Aconite (toxic) (also known as "wolfsbane" and "monkshood"): consecration, purification

Allspice: prosperity, luck, healing, purification, protection, money

Almond: love, money, healing, wisdom

Angelica: protection, hex-breaker, healing, psychic abilities, house blessing, purification

Anise: psychic abilities, lust, luck, purification, love

Apple: love, healing, peace

Ash: protection, strength, healing, prosperity

Basil: discipline, protection, marriage, purification, prosperity, love, luck, mental abilities

Bay leaves: healing, purification, protection, wisdom, psychic abilities, strength

Bayberry: abundance, prosperity

Benzoin: purification, healing, prosperity

Birch: protection, purification, new beginnings, children

41

Calendula: protection, psychic abilities, dreams, success with legal issues, fidelity, healing, love, animals, comfort

Camphor: chastity, sleep, healing

Catnip: love, cats, beauty, happiness, tranquility, luck

Cedar: healing, purification, protection, prosperity

Chamomile: money, love, sleep, meditation, purification, protection, tranquility

Chickweed: animals, love, fidelity, healing, weight loss

Cinnamon: healing, love, lust, success, purification, protection, money, psychic awareness

Cinquefoil (five-finger grass): eloquence, cunning, money, protection, sleep, prophetic dreams, purification, love

Clove: protection, mental abilities, attraction, purification, comfort

Clover: lust, hex breaking, prosperity, purification, love, luck, protection, success, fidelity, comfort

Coffee: energy, grounding

Comfrey (boneset): healing, prosperity, protection, travel

Coriander: healing, love, lust

Cumin: protection, anti-theft, love, fidelity

Cypress: protection, comfort, healing

Daisy: nature spirits, love, children

Damiana: lust, love, psychic abilities

Dandelion: psychic abilities, divination

Dill: protection, love, attraction, money, strength, luck, ease of sleep, mental abilities, weight loss

Dragon's blood: energy, protection, purification, strengthens spells

Echinacea (purple coneflower): healing

Elder, Elderflower: protection from lightning, beauty, divination, prosperity, purification, house blessing, healing, sleep

Elm: love, protection,

Eucalyptus: protection, healing

Eyebright: mental abilities, psychic abilities, clairvoyance, memory

Feverfew: love, fidelity, protection, healing

Flax: money, protection, beauty, healing

Frankincense: protection, purification, meditation

Gardenia: love, attraction, peace, meditation

Garlic: healing, house blessing, protection, lust, anti-theft

Geranium: love, healing, protection, fertility

Ginger: healing, love, money, energy

Hawthorn: protection, fertility, happiness

Hazel: mental abilities, fertility, protection, wisdom, luck

43

Heather: protection, rain, luck

Heliotrope: clairvoyance, psychic abilities, health, money

Hibiscus: love, lust, divination, harmony, peace

High John: prosperity, success, happiness, hex breaker, remove obstacles

Honeysuckle: prosperity, psychic abilities, money

Hops: healing, sleep

Hyacinth: love, comfort, protection

Hyssop: purification, protection

Jasmine: love, attraction, prosperity, tranquility

Juniper: purification, love, protection, health, anti-theft, fertility, psychic abilities

Lavender: love, protection, healing, purification, peace, house blessing, wisdom, children, marriage

Lemon: purification, love, protection, happiness

Licorice: love, lust, protection, fidelity

Lilac: protection, beauty, love, psychic abilities, purification, prosperity

Lily: protection, love antidote, truth

Lime: love, purification, luck, sleep

Lotus: blessing, meditation, protection

Maple: sweetness, prosperity, marriage, love, money

Marjoram: love, marriage, protection, healing, happiness, money, comfort

Mint (see also Peppermint and Spearmint): money, healing, travel, purification, lust

Mistletoe: healing, protection, love, fertility, sleep, luck

Mugwort: travel, divination, psychic abilities, protection, healing, strength, lust

Myrrh: protection, purification, healing, meditation

Neroli (orange blossom): love, marriage

Nettle: protection, healing, lust, hex breaking

Nightshade (toxic) (belladonna): protection

Nutmeg: clairvoyance, health, luck, fidelity

Oak: purification, protection, prosperity, health and healing, money, fertility, luck, strength

Onion: healing, protection, purification

Orange: love, joy, purification, prosperity

Oregano: peace

Orris root: inspiration, purity, love, divination, wisdom, purification, faith, courage

Parsley: healing, lust, fertility, protection, hex breaker, prosperity

Patchouli: money, fertility, lust, clairvoyance, divination, love, attraction

Pepper: protection, purification

Peppermint: healing, love, purification, sleep, psychic abilities, lust

Pine: prosperity, healing, purification, fertility

Poppy: fertility, abundance, sleep, love

Rose: love, fertility, psychic abilities, healing, marriage, luck, protection

Rosemary: mental abilities, memory, anti-theft, purification, healing, sleep, love, lust, protection

Rowan (mountain ash): purification, house blessing, protection, healing, psychic abilities, strengthens spells, wisdom

Rue: protection, mental abilities, purification, health, comfort

Sage: longevity, wisdom, healing, purification, prosperity, business, wishes

Salt: protection, purification, grounding, courage

Sandalwood: protection, healing, meditation, purification

Spearmint: lust, healing, mental abilities, protection at night

St. John's Wort: protection, health, strength, happiness

Strawberry: love, beauty, luck

Sugar: love, sweetness, attraction, friendship

Tea, Black: mental abilities, money, courage, strength

Tea, Green: healing, longevity

Thyme: love, healing, psychic abilities, sleep, purification, courage

Valerian (all-heal): purification, protection, healing, love, sleep, attraction

Vanilla: love, prosperity, lust, energy, mental abilities, creativity

Vervain: creativity, inspiration, purification, healing, divination, protection, prosperity, love, sleep, tranquility

Vetivert: money, love, hex breaking, luck

Violet: tranquility, love, luck, protection, healing

Walnut: healing, mental abilities

Willow: communication, eloquence, protection, healing, love, dreams

Wintergreen: protection for children, hex breaker, healing

Wormwood: removes negative energy, soothes anger, psychic abilities, divination, protection, purification, love

Yarrow: marriage, courage, love and friendship, psychic abilities, hex breaking

Incense and Oils

Name	Magical Properties
Acacia	Psychic powers, Protection
Acorn	Good Luck, personal power, protection, good fortune, wisdom
African Violet	Protection, spirituality, happiness
Agrimony	Strength, protection, renewal, healing. Removal of blockages

Alfalfa	Money and prosperity
Almond	Prosperity and wisdom
Aloe	Cleansing, purification, healing, good luck
Angelica	Protection, healing, courage, divination
Aster	Love, protection, to find lost items, consecration
Basil	Love, Protection, Wealth, prosperity
Bay	Purification, Dreams, Protection, Healing
Bergamot	Money, Protection, restful sleep, love. Increases power of ritual
Birch	Protecting against the evil eye. Purification
Black Pepper	Banishing, protection
Blackberry	Wealth, prosperity, abundance.
Boneset	Protects against curses
Burdock	Removes negative feelings about yourself and others.
Cactus	Banishing and protection. Removes negative blocks
Caraway	Passion, love, protection. Develops concentration and memory
Cardamom	Lust, love, and fidelity
Catnip	Invites good luck

Cedar	Protection, purification, cleansing. Can be used instead of sage when smudging
Chamomile	Cleansing, prosperity. Luck, protection, and banishing
Chervil	Helps to connect with the Higher Self
Chives	Protection. Banishing.
Citronella	Prosperity and luck in business. Cleanses aura.
Clove	Love, prosperity, abundance, and protection
Coriander	Love and lust. Can enhance love and relationships
Cowslip	Blessings for businesses and houses. Promotes youthfulness and vitality
Cumin	Protection, fidelity, exorcism
Cypress	Helps to overcome the loss. Eases grieving
Dandelion	Wealth, prosperity, protection, cleansing. Aids divination
Devils Claw	Protection and banishing
Dill	Wealth attracts money. Blesses houses and keeps away unwanted energy
Dragons Blood	Energy, vitality, dispels negativity
Echinacea	Adds potency to herb mixes
Eucalyptus	Attracts healing energy, aids purification

Evening Primrose	Attracts love and positive energy
Fenugreek	Money and fertility magic
Fig	Aids divination
Frangipani	Attracts love and promotes psychic awareness
Frankincense	Purification, protection, induce psychic powers
Gardenia	Attracts love and friendship. Protects from negative influences
Garlic	Healing, protection, repelling negative energy, purification
Geranium	Harmony and balance. Clears confusion
Ginseng	Love, wealth, vitality, and vibrancy
Gorse	Relationships, romance, love, harmony
Grapefruit	Cleansing and purification
Hawthorn	Fertility, rebirth, renewal, energy
Heather	Brings luck and success
Heliotrope	Joyfulness, prosperity, abundance
Hibiscus	Divination and prophetic dreams. Attracts love
Hyacinth	Love, luck, and good fortune. Promotes restful sleep
Hyssop	Purification and cleansing during rituals

Iris	Promotes wisdom, psychic abilities, self-belief
Ivy	Fertility, love, protection, abundance
Jasmine	Passion, lust, love, and vitality.
Juniper	Attracts good health and prosperity
Kava Kava	Astral travel and protection on the astral planes. Promotes visions
Knotweed	Used in binding spells. Can break curses
Laurel	Luck, protection, and healthy relationships
Lavender	Healing, peace, love, harmony, relaxation
Lemon	Energy, vitality, cleansing, purification
Lemon Balm	Spiritual healing and protection. Aids psychic abilities
Lemongrass	Psychic healing and enhancement of psychic abilities
Lilac	Aids memory and healing. Promotes wisdom
Lily	Death and rebirth. Fertility. Romance and marriages
Lime	Protection and purification
Lobelia	Attracts love, calms conflicts
Lotus	Rebirth, eternal life, fertility, openings
Magnolia	Loyalty, peace, beauty, and love
Maple	Attracts wealth and prosperity. Healing and empowering

Marigold	Good luck in legal matters
Marjoram	Protects against negativity, Draws wealth and abundance
Meadowsweet	Aids friendships. Assists with finding new jobs
Mint	Cleansing, purification, energy, vitality, healing
Mistletoe	Creativity and fertility. Protects against the negative intentions of others
Monkshood	Makes one invisible to enemies. Protection and banishing
Mugwort	Aids with divination and astral travel
Mustard Seed	Enhances courage and faith
Myrrh	Meditation and spiritual awakening. Enhances psychic abilities
Myrtle	Youthfulness, fertility, harmony, and abundance
Narcissus	Peace, tranquility, and harmony
Neroli	Confidence, overcoming blocks, joyfulness
Nettle	Cleansing and protection. Dispels fear and aids courage
Nutmeg	Attracts wealth and abundance, draws luck and prosperity
Oak	Sacred visions and ritual
Olive	Peace, harmony, tranquility
Orange	Energy, vitality, abundance, and prosperity

Orchid	Strengthens willpower, aids focus, and concentration
Oregano	Vitality, joy, prosperity, abundance
Palm	Divination, fertility, willpower, and focus
Papaya	Protects against negativity
Paprika	Adds potency to magical workings, attracts energy and vitality
Parsley	Wealth and prosperity. Aids protection and vitality
Passion Flower	Increases lust, fertility, love, romance
Patchouli	Attracts wealth, abundance, prosperity. Love and passion
Pecan	Wealth, success, career enhancement
Periwinkle	Concentration, focus, and protection. Aids relationships
Pine	Rebirth, Third Eye, moving on after hurts
Pineapple	Luck and success in business
Pomegranate	Fertility, abundance, sacredness, and ritual
Primrose	Encourages the telling of truths. Banishes secrecy
Ragwort	Protection against negativity
Rose	Divine love, romance, relationships, passion, fertility, friendship

Rosemary	Cleansing, energy, purification, protects against nightmares
Rowan	Increases magical powers. Protection and cleansing
Rye	Self-control, fidelity, commitment
Saffron	Wealth, passion, prosperity, healing
Sage	Cleansing, purification, healing, protection, aid healing from grief and loss
Sandalwood	Aids psychic development, meditation, visualization. Cleansing and purification
Senna	Passion, lust, and love
Snapdragon	Purification, protection, cleansing
Sow Thistle	Increases strength and stamina
St. John's Wort	Protects against negativity. Aids sleep and memory
Star Anise	Increases psychic abilities
Sunflower	Protection, vitality, growth
Sweetgrass	Strength, cleansing, purification, seeing spirits
Tansy	Good health, longevity, protection
Tarragon	Aids compassion and self-belief
Tea Tree	Cleansing and purification. Aids concentration and psychic awareness

Thistle	Promotes healing from injuries. Protection from negative energy
Thyme	Protection, healing, loyalty. Promotes strength and courage
Tuberose	Serenity, harmony, and sensuality
Valerian	Aids peaceful visions, purifies scared spaces. Aids love and romantic relationships
Vervain	Protection and peaceful sleep. Enhances creativity
Violet	Calming and soothing. Aids restful sleep and prophetic dreams
Willow	Helps to overcome grief. Calms and soothes nerves. Increases magical abilities
Witch Hazel	Cleansing and protection
Yarrow Flower	Divination, love, happy relationships
Yew	Breaks curses, protection, spiritual cleansing

Chapter 2. What Does It Mean to Be a Witch?

Witches are feared, oppressed, and misunderstood. They are considered the source of every bad thing that goes wrong in reality. From plagues to natural disasters, all of these things are supposedly witches' doing. This is just one aspect of the witch stereotype that is commonly repeated in modern culture with very little evidence to back it up.

Witches are the source of many of today's most popular beliefs, but what exactly does it mean to be a witch? There are some definitions out there, but the dictionary doesn't always offer satisfactory answers. That's because witchcraft is more than just casting spells or practicing magic—it also means being an advocate for more progressive thinking. Witches aren't just women who practice dark arts or have evil intentions; they're activists with a powerful message that all people deserve support.

How do you get started? The simplest way is to find other women who are already practicing witchcraft and ask them for their advice. They will be able to give you specific instructions on how to continue down the path—but they aren't witches because they know how it feels. They've experienced the power of witchcraft, not because they were born this way, but because they chose to embrace it.

What is the essence of witch training? A witch is someone who takes action to make the world a better place. She's not afraid of her anger, because she knows that it's stronger than her fear. A witch knows that there are more powerful things in this world that are more important than what you look like or who your parents are. Witchcraft is more than just learning how to cast spells—it's learning how to think for yourself, trust the universe, and use your own magic to create something spectacular.

What makes a witch different? The most important thing that separates witches from other women is their willingness to stand up for women as a whole and fight against those who try to put them down. A witch doesn't care about what you think, because she knows that the only opinion that matters is her own. When it comes down to it, a witch is someone who dares to be herself and has the wisdom to know what's best for her.

What is a witch's greatest power? The greatest thing about witchcraft is that it gives women the tools they need to take control of their lives. It doesn't matter if you've been abused or beaten down by life; you still can be powerful and confident just like everyone else. That's why witchcraft isn't just something that you practice—it is something that will change your life completely.

What does witchcraft mean to me? Witchcraft is something that has always been around women but didn't get the respect it deserved until recently. It's an act of defiance against anyone who tries to put you down because it means that you say no to the world outside of yourself. A witch is someone who refuses to be defined by anyone or ANYTHING except for herself. It's an act of independence that will change your life in ways that you never imagined.

As a witch, you hold the power to manifest change, but no matter what, you must respect free will. Trying to alter another person's free will can have grave consequences. Be careful when casting spells that include others and be mindful of your intentions.

Chapter 3. Tools for Spells and Witchcraft

In the practice and observance of nearly every religion, there are sacred objects that are incorporated into that religion. It can be in the form of chalices, amulets, candles, shrines with statues of deities to be worshipped, or special clothing worn by the officiants of the religious ceremonies. People like to create and use tools or artifacts in their sacred rituals to create and keep a focus on the spiritual energy in the rituals of their practices.

Wicca is no exception, using many tools in their rituals that all have a specific placement on the altar, a particular use, and a symbolic significance. The tools are used to create a focus on the spiritual energy and to direct it to make a direct connection with the spirit world. There is, however, an important but subtle distinction between the use of symbolic objects by other religions and the use of them by Wiccans. The difference is that Wiccans recognize the fact that they share in nature's powers as co-creators in the power that is given by the Goddess and the God and they are not subject completely to the will and calling of the higher power.

The tools used by Wiccans are both practical and symbolic because each action and each object used and performed in the circle of sacred energy is intended deliberately to direct and harness this force of co-creativity. The tools are used to protect the person and the ritual against unwanted influences of forces of energy, to perform spell work and other works of magic, and to welcome and invoke the energies of the Elements and the deities. The tools themselves have no powers of magic and only work to conduct the personal power of the follower who is using them.

There is no exact set of ritual tools since the tools that are needed will vary depending on the intended use and the tradition. Some solitaries and covens will use a diverse range of objects to observe highly elaborate rituals, while other people and covens will want to keep things more simplified and will use a few tools for multiple functions in the ritual. The tools most commonly thought of as necessities in the practice of Wicca are the censer which is used to hold incense, the athame (a-tha-may) which is the knife used in rituals, the pentacle, the wand, the chalice or cup, and the candle or candle the follower wishes to use. A few other tools that are often mentioned and sometimes used include the ritual scourge, the staff, the sword, the bell, the cauldron, and the broom. It is also considered useful though not mandatory to have altar cloths and decorations, herbs and crystals, a plate for offerings or ritual food, a boline which is a special knife for carving and cutting, and images of the Goddess and God. It is not necessary to compile all of these articles in order to begin your practice. The best way is to begin small and gather your tools one or two at a time until you have collected all of the ones you feel you need. There will be some that you will not ever feel a need to own.

And while it is nice to go out and buy all brand-new items, it is not necessary. Some of the items that you need to collect may already be in your possession being used for other purposes or hidden away in a closet or cabinet. A special or unique goblet or cup that you already own and that has special meaning to you can become your chalice. You can buy items through online shops, but it is also fun to visit resale or second-hand shops where you can feel and touch each individual piece to see if it sends you a particular feeling or energy. If you are artistically inclined, you might be able to make your own tools. Or you may be able to find things in nature that might be used as a tool on your altar. A clean, sterile clamshell that has been cleansed could be an amazing chalice, and a lovely small stick from a special bush or tree can be a great wand. Another way to gather your objects is to create and send out an intention for them and be receptive to their arrival. Do not be impatient in your search but do be receptive to seeing the possibilities in things you see in your everyday life. Don't forget to record in your book what you acquired and when you acquired as tool gathering is an important step in your Wiccan journey.

No matter where or how you find your tools if it is most important that you take the time to cleanse your tools of any unwanted residual energy they may have picked up in their previous environments and to consecrate the tools for your practice of rituals. Even though some tools are purchased new and are promised to have a special consecration, it is still preferred that you cleanse them and instill them with your own energy. Once the tools are cleansed and consecrated it is best to store them in their private place where they can keep their energy safe and not mix it in with the everyday objects that are in your life.

To begin your collection many Wiccans believe it is important to have one tool that represents each of the Elements. You would need to gather an athame for Fire, a wand for Air, a chalice for Water, and a pentacle to represent Earth although you could also use a nice bowl of sea salt. The important thing is that you will feel a special connection and energy to each of the items that you have chosen. So, if a particular tool just doesn't feel right, do not use it. Even though there is a good bit of physical activity in the practice of Wicca, all of the power lies in the energetic connection that the follower has with the divine and the spiritual world.

The Altar

The altar might need to do more than one function in your home, such as acting as a desk or a table, or it might be its own dedicated piece of furniture. Its only real need is that it has a flat top for ceremonial use. It is preferred that the altar is made of a natural material like wood or stone. Any physical object that you have charged with magical energy will be suitable for use as an altar that will contribute to the work of the ritual. If you are performing spell work or rituals outside then try to find an old stump of a tree or a large rock to get as close to nature as possible.

Decorate the altar by using colored fabric or scarves. This method will work particularly well if you find yourself using an everyday piece of furniture or a natural object outdoors. Many Wiccans prefer to follow the colors of the season when putting decorations on their altars, so they might use petals from flowers during the celebration of Spring or holly berries and fir tree sprigs during the season of Yule. Images of deities and crystals and stones are also fine to add as long as you leave the room needed for the tools you will be using.

When you place the tools on the altar there are several ways to lay them out according to the ritual that is being performed. They will also vary according to the various traditions, but there will be some characteristics. One of the types of layouts will divide the altar into two halves. All of the tools will be placed on the left side and will be associated with the Elements of Water and Earth and the Goddess as these are considered to be her Elements. The right side of the altar will be devoted to the Elements of Air, Fire, and God. Another way to lay the altar out is to place the representations of the Goddess and the God in the center of the altar and put the remainder of the tools around them according to the four directions and the Elements. In this method, the tools that are associated with Fire will face South, and the tools that are associated with the Earth will face the North direction.

No matter what tradition you might be following set up the altar to suit your individual tastes and space restrictions. Some people will prefer an elaborate altar arrangement following a specific pattern, and some people will prefer to follow a more eclectic version that uses patterns that resonate with their own individual energy patterns. In addition, while it is nice to have a dedicated space in which to do rituals the kitchen table will work just fine if space is a consideration.

The Athame

This is one of the primary tools for the Wiccan altar. The athame resides in the East which is the direction that represents choice, though, and mind. It can be made of carved stone, wood, or metal since it is not a knife that is used but rather a symbolic symbol. The Athame holds the God or yang energy. They are used to direct energy that is needed for recalling and casting rituals. They are not used to cut any item on the physical plane.

The Bell

The Bell is used to represent the Voice of the Goddess. If you ring the Bell during the ritual, it will bring the attention of the Divine to you and will focus your attention on the Divine. The Bell can be used to call healing energy to you and to clear away any unwanted energy. This is especially useful at the end of a ritual or spell casting but can be done at any time.

The Candle

The altar will commonly hold four candles that are color-coded and stand for each of the four directions. They will be set in the direction they are representing. Blue or aqua is used for the West, orange or red candles stand for the South, white or yellow for the East, and brown, green, or black for the North. If no Goddess or God candles are being used then the center will have candles that are gold, silver, or white. Candles are used to call and hold the Powers that lie in each direction.

When the Goddess or God candles are used, they ate set in the center of the altar or on either side of the Pentacle. Another option is to use a large pillar type of candle to represent the Goddess or to use the three candles to represent the Crone, the mother, and the Maiden which are black, red, and white. The energy of the Divine will be invoked by using these candles.

The Chalice

The chalice represents the Mother Goddess and is one of the most important tools on the Wiccan altar. Any wine-style glass or cup will do just fine, or a fancy ornate version may be used. The only qualifications are that the vessel is curvy or round and holds water. The chalice will be placed on the West side of the altar which is the direction of Water. The chalice will be used for the drink offering in the ceremony, to hold the salt water concoction, or to offer a drink to the Divine.

The Deities

It is always a welcome addition to any altar to have representations or images of the goddesses and gods that are special to you even though these are not technically considered to be tools of the altar. These are there to remind you

65

of the Divinity and they can actually hold energy and vibrations of the Divine. The Divine will dwell on this living temple that your altar has become.

The Plate

Some sort of vessel in which to place offerings to the goddesses and gods will go directly to the center of the altar. This can be in the form of a cup, bowl, or a small dish or plate. If needed the cauldron or chalice may be used for the plate until a suitable plate can be acquired. When the ceremony is finished the offerings will be placed into some form of live water like a lake or a river or buried or poured into the Earth to send them to the Divine.

The Offerings

You will bring to the altar the things you will use to honor the Divine such as a prayer or a small gift. Anything beautiful to you can be used as an offering, such as keeping live flowers on the altar. The offering should not be anything that will bring harm to any living entity because anything that you cause harm to will cause harm to the Divine since the Divine lives in all things. And since the offerings will be returned to the Divine, they should not be things that will harm or have been harmed.

The Pentacle

This five-point star inside of a circle is placed in the center of the altar and serves to offer power and protection to your work in magic.

The Wand

This is just a portable version of the broom. It can be made out of any material that is naturally occurring in nature. Wood is the preferred medium for a wand because wood is naturally occurring in nature and is easy to find and use. The wand is used for channeling magical energy and for divination. In the place of the athame, they can be used to recall and cast circles. On the altar, the wand goes in the South because it represents God, or energy and the transformation and power or magic and will.

The Broom

The broom is not actually an altar tool and would not fit on top of the altar but is nice to have nearby to cleanse the sacred space around the altar.

The Cauldron

A cauldron is a three-legged cast-iron pot used for cooking. Cauldrons are made in all sizes from tiny to huge. They are great for burning things like herbs or incense. The cauldron is one of the most common tools to put on the altar. To create a very uniquely Pagan-inspired incense, place an incense charcoal into the cauldron, cover it with powders or herbs, and light it with fire. Just use caution when burning things anywhere. The legs of the cast iron cauldron will generally keep the heat from reaching what the cauldron is standing on but it never hurts to have some sort of fireproof trivet underneath just in case. The cauldron can also be used to hold brews like complex spells or simple saltwater purifications.

Crystal Ball

This tool is used to represent the Goddess. Wiccans gaze into their crystal ball to have a vision. You can find crystal balls in different sizes and types. However, once you acquire a crystal ball, make sure that you charge it magically as soon as you can. Crystal balls have long been used in witchcraft and other similar practices.

Sensor

This tool is used to hold the incense that you burn during your rituals. You can find sensors in different sizes, shapes, and materials. They are typically made of brass. Nonetheless, you may also use a hanging sensor or a glass tray if it is more convenient for you. A hanging sensor is actually ideal if you wish to disperse the smoke from your incense during your ritual sessions.

Altar Tile

This tool is used as the central area during the ritual process and may contain a pentagram. It is available in different materials. Your altar tile can be of any size, but it is better to have one that fits your altar perfectly. You can also choose to have symbols engraved on it if you want. If your altar tile has a pentagram, see to it that it points upward, not downward.

Jewelry and Accessories

The use of jewelry and accessories is open to many different interpretations. Wiccans are not really required to wear jewelry during a ritual. However, if you wish to wear any celestial symbol or an amulet, you can wear it. You may also wear a bracelet or a ring that features a special gem or stone.

Crystals and Stones

Crystals and Stones are symbols of the natural element Earth. When used in spells and rituals, they represent the North. They are usually used in healing spells. Sometimes, they are used as foundations for pagan altars.

Crystals are living beings that radiate vibration and are capable of lifting your own vibration simply by being within proximity to your body. Crystals can be combined with a number of self-help and healing practices for better results. Some areas where they are finding more usage are meditation, Feng Shui, prayer beads, home or office decoration, energy healing, amulets, baths, fertility and birth, sleep, jewelry, and massage therapy among others. Through all these uses of crystals, their link to health benefits is helpful to humans as well as animals such as your pets and plants too.

Crystals are as valuable as they are numerous. The wide variety of crystals available today makes it possible for a lover of crystals to choose from a range of options. The good thing about crystals is that you can enjoy their health benefits regardless of how you use them. Whether you soak them in your bath water, soak them in the water you drink, wear them as ornaments or amulets, place them in a strategic corner of your room or office, put them under your pillow, or hold them while you meditate, you will always get the same health benefits that crystals are known for when you use them correctly. Normally, each kind of crystal will radiate a particular type of energy that corresponds to and works with the specific energies in certain emotional and physical areas of yourself. Using crystals for healing is as simple as being around them. Other techniques may include holding a crystal in your hand or placing it on a nightstand.

Since these healing crystals are constantly absorbing negative energy to provide healing, they can become blocked. Blockages will then reduce the healing effects of the crystals, hence the importance of cleansing them.

Herbs

Another natural tool that symbolizes the North is ***Herbs***. Even though they come from the earth, when used for spells, each herb may represent a different natural element.

Various Household Items

At certain points and during certain spells, you may need to use items that are usually found around the home. This could be anything from a potted plant, to sea salt, to a piece of string or even just a glass of water. In these instances, it can be possible to use standard, non-magical items. Even those items which are just laying around the home will have their own personal and private energies and these can be turned towards a better use through the practice of Wicca. As practical and natural magic, Wicca has a long history of incorporating the everyday and turning it into the magical. As such, do not be surprised to see even the most mundane object become magical when used correctly.

The Book of Shadows

Keep your Book of Shadows on your altar if possible, or very close by if the altar serves more than one function in your house. You will need it for your rituals and spells and for making notes in it during and after a ritual or a spell.

The most important rule to follow when setting up your altar is to do what feels right to you. It is your altar and only you will use it. If something on the altar does not feel right to you or does not carry the particular energy you want, whether it is stimulating or peaceful, then get rid of that item. If you do not find the item to be meaningful then the Divine will not find it meaningful either. If the altar pleases you then it will please the gods and goddesses.

And remember the tools of the altar are symbolic of the meaning that we give to the ceremonies and the spell castings. The seat of your Power is your heart and you must listen to what it says. If you find a better tool and your Heart says it is so, then use that one. And never use any tool that has negativity tied to it. You might have a beautiful ornate mug in your cabinet that could be used as a chalice, but if the person who gave it to you brings up negative memories or feelings it is a good idea to just get rid of the item. If you associate knives with negative feelings or thoughts then use a beautiful letter opener or similar object for your athame. The goddesses and gods will speak to us in a language we can understand, and each visit from the Divine is particular to the person themselves. And once you have used your tools a few times then you will know those that speak to you with positive energy and those that need to go. What makes your Heart happy is what is right for you.

Consecrating Magic Tools

The first thing you need to know to use any item is to consecrate it. Consecrating an item is a prerequisite for using it in your spells. If the item is not prepared correctly, then the item will not bond properly with your magical energy, and it may become a drain to the spell instead of its intended purpose. Therefore, it is very important to take the time to consecrate your magical tools. When you consecrate your items, you bond with them, and they align themselves to your magical energy. Because of the connection between you and your tools, your magic will become more powerful when you use them. Also, note that you may not need each item in this book. You should try to find which ones speak to you.

Follow the steps below to consecrate your items:

1. Create a magic circle with white chalk or table salt.
2. Draw or place a physical pentacle in the middle of the circle.
3. Put each of the tools on the pentacle, usually in the middle of the pentacle.
4. Put a drop of water and salt on the item.

5. Allow a cloud of incense to pass over the item.
6. Say the following invocation:

Oh, Inana! Oh, Dumuzi!

Bless this tool with your divine hands!

Bless this tool with your honor and glory!

Chapter 4

Chapter 4. Raise Your Energy Before Making a Spell

Let's begin with the question, "What is energy?"

You are surrounded by energy. Everything is made out of energy! You are a source of energy. Your ideas are made up of energy. Everything you perceive is made out of energy. When you comprehend how strong and mystical energy is, it's truly rather amazing.

When we talk about "negative energy" in the spiritual sense, we're talking about undesired energy or energy that doesn't make us feel good. Have you ever stepped into a location and sensed something wasn't quiet, right?

We all have various perspectives on life! What you see as negative energy may be perceived as good energy by someone else. Always pay attention to your gut sensations or intuition. When you sense that the energy in a location or around a certain individual is off, pay attention to the clues your body is sending to you.

Bad emotions (sadness, rage, envy, irritation, etc.) are only some of the things that may cause negative energy to stay in a location. Where there has been a death, wherever there has been any form of violence, a disagreement or a brawl, or sickness or ailment might give you a lot of negative energy too.

It's usually a good idea to purify the area before executing a spell or ritual. This should be performed whether or not you perceive bad energy since not all bad energy is really negative... if that makes sense. Some energy is just unwelcome! For example, if you cast a love spell on Monday and then choose to do money magic on Tuesday in the same spot, the love spell's energy may still be there. This may perplex the cosmos and make manifesting your wishes more difficult.

Witchcraft is a deeply personal path to take. We all practice and develop specific standards of behavior that best suit our personalities over time, but one thing we all have in common is that when we sense that the power in a space is off, we instantly grab our sage, incense, selenite crystal, or whatever cleansing tools we prefer to use to clear the space of that unwanted energy. There are two advantages to purifying a place before a spell or ritual. It will be clear of any unwelcome energy. This will make it easier for you to explain your objectives.

Chapter 5. 100 Spell Jar Recipes

These spells were picked to give you immediate access to spellcasting practice while keeping things at a beginner to intermediate level.

What to Do with Your Spell Jar after the Spell?

This is a good question! You must know what to do with the spell jar when the spell has been completed.

- **Bury That Jar!**

Bury the jar if the jar spell is meant to attract wealth, love, health, and/or prosperity. If the spell is for a business, bury it in a flowerpot inside the building. To protect your own property or self-owned business, bury it on your property or someone else's.

To make it work, you must have land of your own. If you don't have land, use a flower pot. The point is that the vial or jar be buried where it can touch dirt and plant life. You may like to put the jar in a plastic zipper bag before you bury it. It doesn't affect the spell either way. Most witches just prefer the metal and jar to be touching the earth.

- **Habit or Disease**

If you want to rid yourself or someone else of a bad habit, you can bury the jar at a crossroads. Make sure it's an intersection that you or they won't be crossing again in the future, or you'll have to refresh the spell. Again, walk/drive away and don't look back. Extra points if you never return.

77

- **Desperate Times**

Although this is not recommended by most witches, there are times when an action becomes desperate.

You can bury the jar in a cemetery that is not attached to a church. The cemetery can be sponsored by a religious organization, but the building itself must not be in the immediate vicinity.

- o If you were born in January - March, bury the jar in the Northernmost row of the cemetery.
- o If you were born in April - June, bury the jar in the westernmost row of the cemetery.
- o If you were born in July - September, bury the jar in the southernmost row of the cemetery.
- o If you were born in October - December, bury the jar in the easternmost row of the cemetery.
- o Pack the dirt down on the jar and create a salt circle around the edges of the filled-in hole. Don't be stingy with the salt. Don't go on a day when rain is forecast. The salt needs to stay for a full 24 hours!

- **Hide the Jar**

If you want to hide your spell jar, you will need to cover it with a cloth or something similar. That way, only those who know where it is will find it. This is great if you've cast a spell for less stress and the jar needs to be touched and shaken each day. You don't want the spell jar to end up in the wrong hands.

If you have a particularly stubborn curse or spell that you're trying to break, you can use the element of water to help ground the spell and release the energy back into the earth. You can bury the jar near a stream as long as it's legal and there's nothing in the jar that could endanger the ecosystem.

Leave the jar there for one full moon cycle. After a month, go back and get the jar, and then proceed to disassemble the spell.

- **Crossroads**

If you feel a spell has backfired against you or someone else, you can take the jar to an old dirt road and bury the jar according to the birth chart. You should also perform an immediate cleansing ritual and rid yourself and your workspace of all negative energy.

- **Keep the Jar on Your Altar**

If you want to keep the jar on your altar, it should be placed in a place where you will see it every day. It's best to place it somewhere in your home where it won't be disturbed. That way, you'll be able to focus on your spell in the coming days.

- **Don't Smash It or Burn It**

If you burn your spell jar, it will not only lose its power, but you may end up hurting yourself. You must keep your spell jars away from fire and heat sources.

- **Disposing of Old Spells**

Another way of disposing of spell jars or vials is to wrap the entire bottle with twine or ribbon in an X pattern. Then tie the ends together. Place the bundle into a small paper bag. Seal the bag and throw it away. The same goes for any other type of container used for storing magic. This method works well because it keeps the contents safe from harm.

- **Reusing Vials or Jars**

Vials that are used in talismans and amulets can be reused. Jars that are used for spells that require burial should be left alone. You can reuse spell jars that weren't used for protection, money, love, or prosperity. Any others can just have the contents dumped down the drain and can then be washed with warm soap and water.

Remember to bless all your tools after you wash them so that the next time you need them, they're ready to use!

Ready, Set, Go!

Remember to be patient with yourself as you learn. Be prepared for a scorched pot or two, a pan that boils over, and some airing out of the windows when something doesn't smell quite right!

While you prepare the spell, you can begin to think about your intention and the correct wording for the spell. Some general words are included with each spell, but you should try to write your own. The more personal, the better the chance of success!

Love Spell Jar

A Bottle Spell to Strengthen a Relationship

Ingredients:

- ❖ Pen
- ❖ 2 red roses
- ❖ Paper
- ❖ 1 glass bottle with a lid

How to Cast the Spell:

- ❖ Find two red roses, put them in a glass bottle, and put the bottle in the fridge.
- ❖ When you write down the full names of the two people in the couple, put them in a bottle.
- ❖ Then say the spell out loud: Endless-Desire-Bottle-Spell

- ❖ Use a lid or cork to keep the bottle closed.
- ❖ Place it somewhere no one will find it. It could be in your backyard, in a garden, or a wood. Then don't touch it.

Red Candle Spell for Lust & Passion

Ingredients:

- ❖ 4 red candles
- ❖ Honey (1 tablespoon)
- ❖ 1 glass container
- ❖ 1 photo of the couple
- ❖ Sugar (1 tablespoon)

How to Cast the Spell:

- ❖ You can cast this simple spell to bring back the desire and lust in your relationship. The person who does it can be a man or a woman. It will work better if you have a husband, boyfriend, or partner. With red candles, honey, and sugar, you can rekindle the flames of your love again.

- ❖ It will help you become more attractive and sexier to him, even if you know he still loves you. After you try it, your sex frequency should go up a lot.

- ❖ The best time to start this is on a full moon night. Also, this is a spell that you can see both casts. Finally, if you want to stay together and have the best relationship, think of this ritual as a way to start over, a way to start over with love and sex.

Re-Ignite the Passion in Your Relationship

Ingredients:

- ❖ Honey
- ❖ A pinch of thyme
- ❖ 3 Rose petals
- ❖ A pinch of cinnamon or nutmeg
- ❖ A pinch of hibiscus
- ❖ 2 teaspoons of black tea leaves
- ❖ A pinch of Rosemary
- ❖ 3 Pieces of lemon peel
- ❖ A pinch of damiana (or ginseng)

How to Cast the Spell:

- ❖ In a teapot, mix the herbs with 3 cups of boiling water and think about your goals.

- ❖ Allow the tea to steep for a while. As you wait, try to clear your mind and be calm. Think about your partner, picture them next to you, and feel the warmth build up inside of you as you do. They have a face and hands that you like. You can also think of other things about them that you like.

- ❖ Pour the tea into two cups and add honey to make them sweet.

- ❖ With your partner, drink the tea. Sit down. Laugh and talk together. Talk about what you want from the relationship and be open to what the other person has to say.

83

For Love, Peace and Harmony

Ingredients:

- ❖ Gold Glitter

- ❖ Sealable glass bottle or jar

- ❖ Hibiscus - love, protection

- ❖ Bay leaf - healing, protection, and success

- ❖ Herbs (and their relevant qualities)

- ❖ Jasmine - love

- ❖ Roses - love, uplifting

- ❖ Olive Oil (or another carrier)

- ❖ Lavender – happiness, purification

How to Cast the Spell:

- ❖ It's good to light some Sage or Palo Santo, or both.

- ❖ In this way, I will rid this object of any harmful energy so that I can use it for my highest good." You should pick up your glass jar and fan it with the smoke.

- ❖ So, as it is said, so it will be.

- ❖ When you're done with the herbs, glitter, and oil, you can add them all.

- ❖ Shake it very well.

- ❖ Take a look at how all the herbs work together to make a beautiful, harmonizing energy.

- ❖ You can hold it in your heart and thank all the plant spirits who gave you their energy to make this lovely harmonizing oil!

- ❖ That's all! You now have a powerful harmonizing oil that you can use right away.

Now & Forever

Ingredients:

- ❖ 1 picture frame
- ❖ 2 pink candles
- ❖ 1 photo of the couple
- ❖ Your partner's perfume

How to Cast the Spell:

- ❖ They should be on a dish or next to each other. Then, light them up.

- ❖ Make sure the picture is sprayed with your partner's scent before you put it in the picture frame.

- ❖ In this picture, put a frame in front of two candles so that the couple is facing them and getting their light from them.

- ❖ Let go of any worries or fears you have by taking a deep breath in. To reach your goal, you need to keep your mind on it at all. Make a picture of everything you want for your relationship.

- ❖ This spell is: Pink-candle-spell-love

- ❖ During the prayer, say *"So mote it be!"* several times.

- ❖ Keep picturing and focusing on a healthy relationship, and don't let things get in the way. Meditate for a few minutes before you finally put out the lights.

- ❖ Make sure to do this every other day, and use the same candles each time you do it. In time, it will help build up your relationship with each other.

'Gimme' Love Spell Jar

Ingredients:

- ❖ Pink food coloring for romance
- ❖ Dried or fresh lavender for love and protection
- ❖ Orange food coloring for attraction
- ❖ Dried or fresh red or pink roses for love
- ❖ Cinnamon for protection
- ❖ Paper
- ❖ 1 pen/marker with orange ink
- ❖ White sugar for sweetness
- ❖ 1 pink candle

How to Cast the Spell:

- ❖ Fill two bowls with half-white sugar. Add 1 drop of pink food coloring to 1 and 1 drop of orange food coloring to the other one. The sugar in each bowl should be the same color.
- ❖ With a pen and paper, write down the things you want in the person you want to meet. Then put the paper in the bottom of your jar.
- ❖ With a mortar and pestle, mix the roses and lavender while you think about how you want to find love.
- ❖ Stack pink sugar, herb mix, and orange sugar until the jar is full.
- ❖ Sprinkle a little cinnamon on top to make it look like love and happiness are on top.
- ❖ A pink candle can be used to burn over the top of the jar.

New Year, New Me Clarity Jar

Ingredients:

- ❖ Airtight jar
- ❖ Whole cloves for clarity
- ❖ Sea salt (big grain) for protection and cleansing
- ❖ Mint leaves for communication
- ❖ Ground coffee to dispel negative thoughts
- ❖ Whole rosemary sprigs for mental clarity
- ❖ Cinnamon sticks for protection and mental focus
- ❖ 1 orange candle for stimulating your mental energy

How to Cast the Spell:

- ❖ In your jar, put each ingredient on top of the other, and think about how you will use it.

- ❖ Seal the jar and light an orange candle on top.

Spell to Open Roads to Love

Ingredients:

- ❖ Paper and pencil
- ❖ 1 pink candle
- ❖ Candle holder or dish
- ❖ 3 dried white flowers (e.g., daisies, carnations, lilies, tulips, daffodils, or others)
- ❖ Incense (e.g., cinnamon, jasmine, roses, or ylang-ylang)
- ❖ Your cauldron or any fireproof container
- ❖ Essential oil (e.g., cinnamon, clove, jasmine, linden flower, myrtle, orange, palmarosa, rose, vanilla, or yarrow)

How to Cast the Spell:

- ❖ It's time to light the incense and let its scent fill the room.
- ❖ It's time for you to dress up your candle with the essential oil so that you can open the door to the powerful love that changes everything. Do this and say: *Putting love spells on the candle*
- ❖ Make sure the candle is lit and put it on the candle stand or a dish.
- ❖ Take one of the white flowers and gently peel off each petal one by one, making sure not to damage them. During this, breathe slowly and say the following: *Fire-Flower-Spell*
- ❖ Use all three flowers, and put the petals in a pot. Do not worry or think about anything during this time.
- ❖ On the paper, write your full name.
- ❖ It is safe to light the piece of paper with the candle flame and put it in the cauldron.
- ❖ It's OK to let the candle burn and put

90

its ashes in the
flowerpot as you say.
Thanks.

❖ Take the ashes and
the last petals from
the cauldron and
bury them in the
ground (in a garden
or flower pot).

Self-Love & Spiritual Acceptance

Ingredients:

- 8 rose petals (fresh or dried)
- 1 white candle
- 2 tablespoons of Cinnamon powder

How to Cast the Spell:

- In a pot, put 4 cups of water. Then, put the pot on a stove over high heat.

- Add the rose petals and cinnamon to the dough and mix it well.

- Turn off the heat when it starts to boil. Let it sit for about 15 minutes before you start to eat it

- Meanwhile, take a quick shower to clean your body. Then, fill the tub with warm water and get in there.

- It's time to light a white candle. Add the rose petals, cinnamon, and water to the water.

- As you pour the water on your body and face, think about why your heart is hurting. You should not only think about what other people have done to you. You should also think about how you have treated your own body.

- Thank yourself and ask that all bad thoughts go away. Take note of the things that your emotions are trying to say. Your fears will help you figure out what to do, Self-Love-Spell-Bath

- Get out of the tub when you're ready and do what makes you happy.

Self-Love Bath

❖ Bath magic is ideal for cleansing away old energy and for allowing new, nurturing energy to take root. This spell is perfect for generating more self-love for your physical, mental, emotional, psychological, and spiritual self.

❖ *When to Perform This Spell:* On a Monday, Friday, or during a full moon
❖ *Time to Allot for the Spell:* 30 minutes
❖ *Where to Perform the Spell:* Bathroom

Ingredients/Tools:

❖ 1 cup Epsom salt

❖ 3 drops of jasmine essential oil
❖ 3 drops of rose essential oil
❖ Lighter or matches
❖ Pink pillar candle
❖ Rose quartz crystal

Steps:

❖ Cleanse your bathroom.
❖ Fill your bathtub with warm or hot water.
❖ Add the Epsom salt and jasmine and rose essential oils.
❖ As the tub fills, light the candle and set it in a safe location nearby.
❖ Hold the rose quartz in your dominant hand and soak it in the bath for 20 minutes. Focus on the things you love

about yourself. Feel the bathwater infuse your body and the rose quartz with love and healing energies.

❖ After 20 minutes, drain the bath and blow out the candle.

❖ Whenever you need a boost of self-love, light the candle and hold the rose quartz.

Getting Over Love Spell

This spell will help you move on from past love. The ideal time to cast this spell is after a full moon, once the moon begins to wane back into the darkness of the new moon.

When to Perform This Spell: During a waning moon

Time to Allot for the Spell: 15 minutes

Where to Perform the Spell: Altar

Ingredients/Tools:

- 3 drops of clove essential oil
- 1 tablespoon olive oil
- Small dish
- Black pillar candle
- Lighter or matches
- Pen and paper
- Large bowl
- Small bowl
- About ½ cup of water

Steps:

- Cleanse your altar. Mix the clove essential oil and olive oil in a small dish. Using your fingers, anoint your black candle. Be careful not to get oil on the wick.
- Light the candle and focus on your intentions to cut ties with your ex-lover.
- Write a goodbye message to the feelings that no longer serve you. Put the message in a large bowl.
- Fill a small bowl with water and place your hands into it, cleansing away pain, anger, and resentment.
- Lift some water out of the bowl with your hands and throw it on the paper, enforcing your goodbye.
- Squeeze the paper and discard it, removing it from your life.
- Whenever you feel old feelings returning, light your anointed candle.

Custom Love Sigil

Creating a custom love sigil is fun and creative! This sigil is perfect for drawing more attention to you from your love interest. It's also the perfect way to illuminate your true feelings.

When to Perform This Spell: On a Friday or during a new moon

Time to Allot for the Spell: 10 minutes

Where to Perform the Spell: Altar

Ingredients/Tools:

- ❖ 2 sheets of paper
- ❖ Pen with red ink

Steps:

- ❖ Cleanse your altar.
- ❖ Write your name and your love interest's name on one of the sheets of paper with a red pen.
- ❖ Deconstruct the letters of the names into their basic strokes, like curves, dots, dashes, and lines. Draw these strokes below the names on the same paper.
- ❖ Still, on the same sheet of paper, combine the strokes to form the outline of a shape. This could be a square, a heart, a cross, or a triangle. Place any remaining circles, arcs, and dashes along the lines or around the shape. This shape is your love sigil.
- ❖ Redraw your love sigil, now coded with your intentions, on the second sheet of paper. Carry it with you.

96

Restore Love Knot Spell

Did you have an argument with your loved one that you regret? Do you want to bring your romance back to the beginning? This spell is perfect for returning the energy of your relationship back to how it was when the love was pure and new.

When to Perform This Spell: On a Monday or during a new moon

Time to Allot for the Spell: 45 to 60 minutes

Where to Perform the Spell: Altar

Ingredients/Tools:

- Desire Incense or Positivity Incense
- Charcoal disc and heat-proof dish (optional)
- 3 red tea light candles
- Lighter or matches
- 2 (12-inch) pieces of string in different colors

Steps:

- Cleanse your altar.
- Burn your Desire or Positivity Incense. If your incense is loose, burn it on a charcoal disc on a heat-proof dish. Set up the candles in a triangular configuration.
- Light the candles and focus on your intention of restoring love.
- Hold the two strings together and tie a simple overhand knot at one end. As you do this, say, *"Knot of love, revive what has vanished."*
- Tie another knot and say, *"Knot of passion, bring back the delight."*
- Tie the third knot and say, *"Knot of adoration, renew what was damaged."*
- Tie a fourth and final knot and say, *"Knot of desire, mend and rewrite."*
- Allow the candles to burn while you meditate, visualizing the love you want to be restored. Continue until 45 to 60 minutes have passed.

Burning Heartbreak Spell

Burn away heartbreak using the element of fire. This spell uses photographs and lemon balm, which is known for its healing properties. It will help you recover from the emotional pain of a broken relationship.

When to Perform This Spell: On a Monday or during a dark moon

Time to Allot for the Spell: 30 to 45 minutes

Where to Perform the Spell: Altar or outdoor firepit

Ingredients/Tools:

- ❖ Outdoor firepit, if outside
- ❖ Fire-safe bowl, if indoors at your altar
- ❖ Lighter or matches
- ❖ 2 photographs, one of you and another of the person who broke your heart
- ❖ A small handful of dried lemon balm
- ❖ Sea salt (optional)

Steps:

- ❖ Cleanse your altar or outdoor firepit area.
- ❖ If performing the spell indoors, use a lighter to ignite the edge of each photo before placing it inside your fire-safe bowl. If spellcasting outside, you may toss each photo one at a time into the fire. As the photographs burn, say:

"With this photo, I ease my sorrow; with this fire, I burn away this grief; with these ashes, I take away this pain."

- ❖ When you have burned both of your photos, toss the lemon balm into the fire or the bowl.
- ❖ Optional: Collect some of the ash from the fire and mix it with sea salt to create a powerful nonedible black salt that can be sprinkled or thrown around you to banish negative emotions in the future.

Mending Heartbreak Talisman

This spell will teach you how to create a talisman that will assist your heart's healing. Your talisman must be worn at all times. This recipe uses cayenne pepper, which provides support during separations and emotional heartache.

When to Perform This Spell: On a Monday or during a dark moon

Time to Allot for the Spell: 15 minutes

Where to Perform the Spell: Altar

Ingredients/Tools:

- ❖ Pinch of cayenne pepper
- ❖ Black or white votive or pillar candle
- ❖ Lighter or matches
- ❖ Necklace

Steps:

- ❖ Cleanse your altar.
- ❖ Sprinkle the cayenne pepper on the top of the candle to anoint it.
- ❖ Light the candle and visualize its mending properties.
- ❖ Move your necklace through the candle's smoke as you say,

"Necklace of healing, fill the void of my broken heart, as I imbue you with energy and feeling; support me in creating my restart."

- ❖ Allow your power to infuse the necklace, charging it for use.
- ❖ Repeat the spell every few months to recharge

the talisman. You may
use the same candle.

Charm for Attracting Quality Relationships

This spell draws on both the attracting and protective qualities of coriander for a balanced approach to attracting new potential partners into your life.

This is particularly good for those who seem to have no trouble attracting admirers, but plenty of trouble in the relationships that develop. With the energy of coriander, people who are ultimately no good for you will not make it into your sphere of awareness, while people who present a positive, healthy, compatible match will have a clear path to you.

Adding rose quartz to the mix enhances the positive vibration of the spell. Be sure to get whole seeds rather than coriander powder, since you'll be carrying the herb with you.

You will need:

- ❖ 13 whole coriander seeds
- ❖ 1 small rose quartz
- ❖ 1 small drawstring bag or piece of cloth
- ❖ 1 red or pink ribbon
- ❖ 1 work candle (for atmosphere—optional)

Instructions:

- ❖ Light the candle, if using.
- ❖ Arrange the coriander seeds in a circle around the rose quartz.
- ❖ Close your eyes and visualize the feeling of being completely at peace with a partner who loves you for exactly who you are.
- ❖ When you have a lock on this feeling, open your eyes, focus on the rose quartz, and say the following (or similar) words:

"I draw to be nothing less than healthy, balanced love."

- ❖ Now collect the coriander seeds, placing them one at a time into the drawstring bag or cloth. (It's best to start with the seed at the

102

southern-most part of
the circle and move
clockwise.)

❖ Add the rose quartz,
close the bag or cloth,
and secure with the
ribbon.

❖ Bring the charm with
you whenever you're
feeling like taking a
chance on love—
especially when you go
out in public.

Romance Attraction Smudge

This is a fun, simple ritual for enhancing the atmosphere in your home or any space where you'd like to encourage romance!

You will need:

- ❖ 1 red candle
- ❖ Sprig of dried lavender or lavender-only smudge stick
- ❖ Rose essential oil (optional)
- ❖ 1 feather (optional)

Instructions:

- ❖ Anoint the candle with a drop or two of the rose oil, if using. Wipe away any excess oil from your fingers, and then light the candle.
- ❖ Ignite the lavender sprig or smudge stick from the candle flame as you say the following (or similar) words:

"Loving lavender, creative fire, charge this space with love's desire."

- ❖ Starting at a point in the northern part of the room, move in a clockwise circle, fanning the lavender smoke with the feather (if using) or your hand, so that it spreads throughout the room as much as possible. If you like, you can repeat the words of power above as a chant as you go.
- ❖ Leave the lavender to burn out on its own in a fire-proof dish, if possible—otherwise, you can extinguish it gently in a potted plant or bowl of sand.

Stellar First Date Confidence Charm

If you're the type who gets nervous before meeting a potential love interest for the first time, this spell is for you.

Simply carry the charm with you in your pocket or purse—you may want to enclose it in a drawstring bag or cloth if you're carrying it with other items to keep it intact.

Keep in mind that the focus here is on your own confidence and sense of self-love no matter what the *other person is like.* If you have a good time, no matter what the outcome, then the spell has been a success.

You will need:

- ❖ 1 pink or white ribbon, about seven inches
- ❖ 1 little piece of carnelian or tiger's eye
- ❖ Sea salt
- ❖ 1 work candle (optional)
- ❖ 1 little drawstring bag or piece of cloth (optional)

Instructions:

- ❖ Light the candle, if using.
- ❖ Lay out the ribbon on your altar or work space.
- ❖ Create a circle of sea salt around the ribbon—this will concentrate the energy of the spell around the charm.
- ❖ Place the stone on the ribbon, and say the following (or similar) words:

"My confidence radiates from within, I am comfortable in my own skin, this meeting of souls will be a pleasure, I charm this stone for extra measure."

- ❖ Tie the ribbon gently around the stone and secure it with a knot.
- ❖ Now go out and have fun meeting someone new!

Ritual Bath for a Blind Date

Whether you're on a blind date set up by a friend, or taking the plunge into the world of online dating, it can be nerve-wracking to meet someone new.

This spell makes it nearly impossible not to have a good time, by sublimating nervousness and promoting self-confidence, which will improve the energy of the encounter no matter what the outcome. Indeed, you will enjoy yourself even if it's clear by the end that there won't be a second date!

You will need:

- ❖ 1 teaspoon to 1 tablespoon hibiscus
- ❖ 1 teaspoon to 1 tablespoon chamomile
- ❖ 1 teaspoon to 1 tablespoon coltsfoot or red clover
- ❖ 2 to 3 tablespoons Himalayan salt or sea salt
- ❖ 5 drops of lavender essential oil
- ❖ 1 citrine, aventurine, or tiger's eye
- ❖ Candle(s) for atmosphere

Instructions:

- ❖ Run the bath until the tub is a quarter of the way full, and add the salt.
- ❖ When the tub is halfway full, place the crystal of your choice in the water, and add the oil.
- ❖ When the bath is almost full, add the herbs.
- ❖ Light the candle(s), turn off any artificial lighting in the bathroom, and climb in.
- ❖ Relax and consciously release any anxiety you may be feeling about meeting this new person. Also, release any attachments you may be feeling to the desired outcome.
- ❖ Stay in the bath for at least 20 minutes. If you can, remain in the tub while draining the water, as the energy of the herbs and crystal

tends to have a stronger
effect that way.
❖ Bring the crystal with
you on the date, and
have a good time!

Rose Attraction Potion

This potion is ideal for attracting potential new suitors or admirers into your life. It involves easy-to-find herbs and tools that you likely already have in your home. A rose is the best flower to use in this recipe due to its association with love.

When to Perform This Spell: On a Friday or during a waxing moon

Time to Allot for the Spell: 15 minutes

Where to Perform the Spell: Kitchen

Ingredients/Tools:

- Small pot
- 1 cup water
- 1 teaspoon dried rose petals
- 1 teaspoon dried hibiscus flowers
- 1 teaspoon dried lavender flowers
- Pinch of cinnamon
- Muslin cloth or strainer
- Cup for drinking

Steps:

- Cleanse your kitchen.
- In a small pot, boil the water as you set your intentions.
- Remove the pot from the heat. Place the rose petals, hibiscus, lavender, and cinnamon one at a time into the pot. As you do this, repeat the words *"Infuse, imbue, impart, immerse"* four times.
- Slowly stir the mixture as you visualize the energy of attraction wrapping around the herbs in the pot. Allow the potion to steep for 10 minutes.
- Strain the potion into a cup and drink.

Lovers' Bind Rune

Preserve or attract a loving relationship with the help of this bind rune. Bind runes are made by combining two or more runes into a single shape. To perform this spell, find a flat stone that calls to you. You'll use this stone to house your bind rune.

When to Perform This Spell: On a Friday or during a new moon

Time to Allot for the Spell: 15 minutes

Where to Perform the Spell: Altar

Ingredients/Tools:

- List of runes and their meanings
- Sheet of paper
- Red permanent marker
- Foraged stone or rock, flat enough to write on

Steps:

- Cleanse your altar.
- Practice creating a bind rune by drawing two rune shapes on top of one another on a sheet of paper. Choose two runes that represent your intention of love. For relationships and happiness, Gebo and Wunjo are great runes to use. Gebo is the rune of gifts and partnerships, and Wunjo is the rune of joy and pleasure.
- Purify the stone.
- Hold the stone in your hand and visualize the energy of your intentions pouring into the stone.
- Use the permanent marker to write the bind rune on your stone.
- Carry your bind rune charm with you.

109

Candle Melding Love Spell

When the candles begin to melt, and the wax melds together, you and your partner will be drawn to one another once more.

You will need

- ❖ 2 red candles that are shaped like humans
- ❖ Some ginger oils

Instructions:

- ❖ If you can't find any red candles shaped as figures, just use standard candles, so long as they are red. Smear the ginger oil over both candles and then place them in a dish together. They must be in the same dish, not in separate ones, as the candles have to be touching.
- ❖ Light both candles and focus on the positive thoughts of your partner as the wax begins melting. Let the wax from the candles run into each other and focus on the spell and your partner until the candles are sufficiently melted to join together. Repeat the following words until you feel you have got your message across to the universe.

"Candles burn, and wax will run, You and I again are one."

❖ Leave the candles to burn out by themselves.

Return to Me Candle Spell

This is another powerful spell that can help you and your partner reunite.

You will need

- ❖ Some red yarn or string
- ❖ Some vanilla oil
- ❖ 1 candle, either red, white, or pink

Instructions:

- ❖ Inscribe the candle with your initials or your full name using a sharp implement. Above yours, in the center of the candle, inscribe your partner's name or initials, ensuring you write over the top of the first letters.
- ❖ Smear oil on the candle and then tie the red yarn around it. Tie it in a bow, making sure the knot is above the initials. Light it and leave it to burn until the flame is getting close to the top carving. Extinguish the candle

and leave it near your altar, letting the universe know that your spell will be completed when your partner has returned to you. Every day, rub more oil over the initials, only stopping when you are reunited.

Money and Prosperity Spell Jar:

Spell to Create a Consciousness of Prosperity

Before you can attract wealth, you have to feel that you are worthy of it. Many of us have been taught to believe we do not deserve prosperity, but those ideas can hinder your ability to achieve financial security.

You will need:

- 14 green votive candles
- Pine Essential Oil
- 1 empty glass container
- A piece of paper

Instructions:

- The first night of this spell should be a new moon.
- Anoint and dress the green candles with the pine essential oil.
- Write your affirmations (desires) on the piece of paper.
- On the night of the new moon, light one of the candles. While it is burning, read your affirmation aloud. Focus on the feeling that it is already done, that your affirmation has already been met.
- After approximately 5 minutes, snuff the candle. Rub your hands in the smoke and waft the smoke toward your face, your body, and your clothes. Lock that scents into your mind so you associate the scent with abundance, prosperity, and your belief.

- ❖ Repeat this ritual each day for the next 13 days, using a new candle each time. Keep the spent candles with each other and separate from the unused candles.

- ❖ On the night of the full moon, after having performed this spell for fourteen straight days, light all fourteen candles again (all together). Let the candles burn themselves out.

- ❖ Collect the remnants of the candles and place them in the glass jar. Also, place your written affirmation into the jar. Bury the jar in the front yard of your home.

Elemental Money-Drawing Spell with Sea Salt

Ingredients:

- ❖ Dish
- ❖ Sea salt
- ❖ Seashells
- ❖ 2 green candles
- ❖ 1 white candle
- ❖ Incense stick (any essence, e.g., patchouli, frankincense, etc.)

How to Cast the Spell:

- ❖ You can put a dish in the middle of your altar. Three candles: One white candle and two green ones. Place them on the dish together.

- ❖ Light up your incense stick, and you'll smell better. Add seashells to the dish, either on top of or around it. The more you use, the better! Using sea salt, cover the dish and shells with a circle around them all.

- ❖ They need to be lit up, so You can use this spell to get what you want in your life. Spend a few minutes focusing all of your energy on what you want. Make a list of what you need and why.

- ❖ Visualize exactly what you want to do, and feel happy, satisfied, or grateful when you think about it. Think about what you want so you can feel it as if it's already there.

- ❖ Take another handful of sea salt and put it on top of

the seashells as you do this. Then say this chant: Salt-Money-Prayer-Spell

❖ To let the candles burn, you should make sure the wax and salt are out when they are done. Then throw them outside. Throw them in a river or somewhere where water flows. Otherwise, you can bury them or put them in the compost/trash if you don't want to use them.

❖ Keep the seashells in your bedroom, where you can see them every day and think about how much money is coming your way. This will help you remember that money is coming your way.

116

Money Bags: A Powerful Spell with Cinnamon and Coins

Ingredients:

- ❖ String or thread
- ❖ Green cloth
- ❖ 1 green candle
- ❖ Cinnamon powder (or ground cinnamon)
- ❖ 6 coins of any value
- ❖ A prosperity oil (such as patchouli, bergamot, cinnamon, myrrh, sandalwood, or ginger)

How to Cast the Spell:

- ❖ Place all of the ingredients on your altar, take a few deep breaths, and start making your own altar. Make sure you have a clear and positive mindset for the rite.

- ❖ Dress the candle with the oil you've chosen, then light it. If you've never done this before, put some oil on your fingers and rub the candle up and down while you think about your goal of bringing money into your life.

- ❖ Place the candle on a dish or candle holder on your altar and then light it up.

- ❖ A circle with six coins around a candle. As you do this, use your mental energy to think about how thankful you are for the money.

- ❖ Chant this money-drawing spell three times. Chant a prayer for money.

- ❖ Place the green cloth on your altar, sprinkle some cinnamon, and then light a candle.

- For each of the six coins, say these words: *Money that comes to me is like a spell.*

- It's a good idea to take the ends of the green cloth and tie them together to make a small pouch.

- This is your money-drawing charm. Take it with you at all times. You could put it in your purse, bag, or pocket at all times. Every time you see it, picture yourself getting the money you want.

Money Manifestation Spell in the Full Moon

Ingredients:

- ❖ Water
- ❖ Cauldron (or a regular bowl)
- ❖ 1 quarter (or a similar coin)

How to Cast the Spell:

- ❖ On a full moon night, put drinking water in your cauldron or a bowl that you can use for other things.

- ❖ It's time to make some magic. Put a quarter in the water and put the pot on a window curtain or a table where the full moon will shine.

- ❖ Chant three times: The Full Moon Money Spell, Leave the water out all night.

- ❖ The next morning, remove the quarter. Make sure the new soil is wet before you do this.

- ❖ You should do this for a week: Keep the quarter in your pocket or purse. After that, use it. This way, you give it away to the Universe and bring money into your life.

'Moon Boon Chant': Wiccan Magic to Attract Money

Ingredients:

- ❖ Glass bowl
- ❖ Sugar
- ❖ 1 small glass
- ❖ Water
- ❖ 1 bill of any value and currency

How to Cast the Spell:

- ❖ Put your tools near a window where the full moon will shine when it's dark outside.

- ❖ Add some tap water to a glass bowl. Put it on the table.

- ❖ Pour some sugar into a small glass.

- ❖ In a bowl of water, put the glass with the sugar inside. This way, the water won't touch the sugar. Under the bowl, put the bill.

- ❖ Whisper the spell: Chant the Full Moon Money.

- ❖ Overnight, leave it outside. Take it inside the next day before the sun hits it.

- ❖ Take the bill and put it in your wallet or purse as an amulet to keep you safe.

- ❖ Water and sugar should be mixed. Pour it into a small hole in the ground or a flower pot with soil.

Spell to Attract Prosperity

This prosperity spell can be used for any kind of prosperity - financial gain or prosperity in the fullness of inner peace, the source of all true prosperity.

You will need:

❖ 1 green candle

❖ 1 sprig of white sage

❖ A pinch of cinnamon

❖ A cauldron or metal bowl

Instructions:

❖ On the night of the new moon, put the green candle and the white sage in the cauldron or bowl.

❖ Light both the candle and the sage.

❖ Sprinkle cinnamon into the flame of the candle.

While you do so, recite the following,

"I embrace prosperity and inner peace."

❖ Repeat these words and keep sprinkling cinnamon into the flame until the cinnamon is gone.

Cauldron Manifestation Spell

There are times when your desired manifestation may take longer than others. Do not be discouraged. Remember that the universe will provide in its own time. While you wait, try this spell to nurture your wish and bring it to fruition.

You will need:

- ❖ 1 piece of paper
- ❖ A pair of scissors
- ❖ A cauldron or metal bowl
- ❖ A pinch of powdered ginger
- ❖ 1 capsule or tablet of 'Blessed Thistle'
- ❖ A piece of green cloth

Instructions:

- ❖ Cut the sheet of paper into 12 strips. On one strip, write your wish in the form of an affirmation.

- ❖ Fold the paper trip three times and put it in the cauldron.

- ❖ Sprinkle the powdered ginger in the cauldron, along with the broken Blessed Thistle herbal supplement.

- ❖ Cover the cauldron or bowl with the green cloth.

- ❖ Let the cauldron or bowl sit overnight.

- ❖ In the morning, remove the cloth and repeat the spell.

- ❖ Continue in this manner for a total of 12 days.

- ❖ **Note:** If your desire has not yet materialized by the time of the full moon, take a break from the spell during the waning moon and begin again on the first day of the waxing moon. Do not give up! Trust that the universe will provide when the time is right.

Money Powder

This powder is great for improving any kind of financial situation. Sprinkle it around yourself to invite more money to come to you at home, at work, or while gambling. You can also burn money powder on a charcoal disc on a heat-proof dish to increase the power of other prosperity and money spells.

When to Perform This Spell: On a Thursday or during a waxing moon

Time to Allot for the Spell: 15 minutes

Where to Perform the Spell: Altar or kitchen

Ingredients/Tools:

- ❖ Mortar and pestle or grinder
- ❖ 1 tablespoon dried chamomile
- ❖ 1 tablespoon cinnamon
- ❖ 1 tablespoon dried cloves
- ❖ 1 tablespoon dried parsley
- ❖ Funnel
- ❖ Glass vial or jar with a lid

Steps:

- ❖ Cleanse your altar or kitchen space.
- ❖ With the mortar and pestle, grind the chamomile, cinnamon, cloves, and parsley, setting a specific intention to attract money into your life.
- ❖ As you grind the mixture into a powder, say the following four times:

"Growing riches, sprouting funds."

- ❖ Use a funnel to pour the powdered herbs into a glass vial.
- ❖ Your powder is charged and ready for use.

Riches Sigil

Creating a custom money sigil can help you attract wealth and riches. To get started with this simple spell, all you need is your imagination, intention, and something to write with. Using a green pen will help elevate your spell.

When to Perform This Spell: On a Sunday, Thursday, or during a waxing or new moon

Time to Allot for the Spell: 10 minutes

Where to Perform the Spell: Altar

Ingredients/Tools:

- ❖ Pen with green ink
- ❖ 2 sheets of paper

Steps:

- ❖ Cleanse your altar.
- ❖ Use a green pen to write the phrase Bring me riches on the first sheet of paper. Focus on your intentions.
- ❖ Deconstruct the letters of the phrase into basic strokes, like curves, dots, dashes, and lines. Draw these strokes below the phrase on the same paper.
- ❖ On the same sheet of paper, combine the strokes to form the outline of a shape. This could be a square, a heart, a cross, or a triangle. Place any remaining circles, arcs, and dashes along the lines or around the shape. This shape is your money sigil.
- ❖ Redraw your money sigil, now coded with your intentions, on the second sheet of paper. Carry it with you.

Income Moon Water Spell

When to Perform This Spell: During a full moon

Time to Allot for the Spell: 15 minutes

Where to Perform the Spell: Outdoors, preferably under the moonlight

Ingredients/Tools:

- 3 coins
- ½ cup water
- Small bowl
- 4 citrine crystals
- Funnel
- Small glass jar

Steps:

- Cleanse your outdoor altar space.
- Purify the coins to remove unwanted or old energies.
- Add the water to the bowl. Arrange the citrine crystals in a diamond shape around the bowl.
- Place the purified coins into the bowl of water and chant,

- "Glowing moon, charge and infuse;
- glistening coin, be the muse;
- gleaming water, now transfuse."
- Allow the crystals and water to get a full charge. Then, use a funnel to transfer the water into a glass jar.
- Your citrine crystals and moon water are now ready. Use the citrine to create a Prosperity Talisman or as a charm. Use the full moon–charged water to bless your spells involving plants, offerings, or baths.

Wealth Manifestation Rice

We all sometimes need to manifest some extra wealth in our lives. This spell makes use of rice for its attributes relating to money and prosperity. The roots of this spell stem from folk magic.

When to Perform This Spell: During a new moon or waxing moon

Time to Allot for the Spell: 15 minutes, plus 12 hours to dry

Where to Perform the Spell: Kitchen

Ingredients/Tools:

- ❖ 1 cup uncooked jasmine rice
- ❖ 2 medium bowls
- ❖ 1 tablespoon Income Moon Water
- ❖ 1 teaspoon green food coloring
- ❖ Paper towels
- ❖ ¼ cup shredded dollar bills
- ❖ 1 tablespoon cinnamon
- ❖ Large glass jar with a lid

Steps:

- ❖ Cleanse your kitchen.
- ❖ Purify the rice.
- ❖ In a medium bowl, thoroughly mix the rice, Income Moon Water, and green food coloring, focusing on your intentions.
- ❖ Pour the mixture onto paper towels. Let dry for about 12 hours.
- ❖ In another medium bowl, combine the dried green rice mixture with the shredded dollar bills and cinnamon. Pour the mixture into a large glass jar and close the lid.
- ❖ Sprinkle your Wealth Manifestation Rice around you or carry some as a charm.

Luxury Tea Materialization Spell

During stressful financial times, brewing a cup of tea can be a useful ritual. With this minty spelled tea, you can transport yourself to luxury. This quick spell can be used anytime you want to materialize luxury in your life. All you need is a bit of mint and some common kitchen items.

When to Perform This Spell: On a Sunday or during a new moon

Time to Allot for the Spell: 15 minutes

Where to Perform the Spell: Kitchen

- ❖ *Ingredients/Tools:*
- ❖ Small pot
- ❖ 1 cup water
- ❖ 1 tablespoon dried mint or 2 tablespoons fresh mint
- ❖ Muslin cloth or strainer
- ❖ Cup for drinking

Steps:

- ❖ Cleanse your kitchen.
- ❖ In a small pot, boil the water as you set your intentions.
- ❖ Remove the pot from the heat.
- ❖ If using fresh mint, take the leaves in your hands and smack them to awaken their scent. Add the mint to the pot. Let steep for 10 minutes while meditating on your intentions.
- ❖ Strain the tea into a cup. Move your hand in a clockwise direction, and say,

"I mixed this brew to obtain what I require, and filled this cup to secure what I desire."

- ❖ Feel the energy fusing with your tea. Drink and enjoy.

Milk and Honey Money Bath Ritual

Healthy finances start with the right mindset. This ritual bath can clear away your money worries and fears, allowing healthy energy to take root. Perform this ritual before any money spell to reset your intentions and energy.

When to Perform This Spell: On a Sunday, Thursday, or during a new moon

Time to Allot for the Spell: 45 minutes

Where to Perform the Spell: Bathroom

Ingredients/Tools:

- ❖ 2 cups whole milk
- ❖ ½ cup honey
- ❖ Large bowl
- ❖ Lighter or matches
- ❖ White pillar candle

Steps:

- ❖ Cleanse your bathroom.
- ❖ Fill your bathtub with warm or hot water.
- ❖ As the tub fills, stir together the milk and honey in a large bowl, focusing on your intention to revive your finances.
- ❖ Light the candle and set it in a safe location nearby.
- ❖ Pour the milk and honey mixture into the bathtub.
- ❖ Soak in the bath for 30 minutes. Focus on resetting your mindset about your money. Clear away fears and worries.
- ❖ After 30 minutes, drain the bath and blow out the candle.
- ❖ Perform this ritual as often as needed.

Fortune Apple Pomander Spell

Apples can bring fortune into your life in the form of property, assets, resources, possessions, and prosperity. This pomander spell takes about three weeks to work its magic, and when it's finished, it makes for a strong magical charm.

When to Perform This Spell: During a new moon

Time to Allot for the Spell: 20 minutes on the first day, then 5 minutes every day for 3 weeks

Where to Perform the Spell: Altar

Ingredients/Tools:

- Lighter or matches
- Green candle
- Wooden or metal skewer
- Green apple
- 20 whole cloves
- 1 teaspoon cinnamon
- 1 teaspoon nutmeg
- 1 teaspoon ginger
- 1 teaspoon allspice
- 1 teaspoon orris root (optional)

- Small bowl

Steps:

- Cleanse your altar.
- Light the candle while focusing on your intentions.
- Use the skewer to poke holes into your apple, making sure the holes are large enough to fit whole cloves.
- Fill the holes with whole cloves. As you do this, say aloud the fortunes you wish to bring into your life.
- In the bowl, combine the cinnamon, nutmeg, ginger, allspice, and orris root and place it on your altar.
- Roll the clove-filled apple in the bowl of spices for 5 minutes every day for three weeks. As you roll your apple, meditate on your intentions. This will allow your apple to dry (rather than shrivel) and become infused with your intentions.
- Keep your spelled apple pomander on your altar.

Money Grow Dressing Oil

Do you wish that you could multiply your money? Rub this oil mixture on your skin to help you stay focused so you can improve your finances. Remember to do a patch test first if you have sensitive skin. You can also dress your candles or tools with this oil to enhance the power of other money spells.

When to Perform This Spell: On a Thursday or during a waxing moon

Time to Allot for the Spell: 15 minutes

Where to Perform the Spell: Altar

Ingredients/Tools:

- Small amber roller bottle or dropper bottle
- 2 tablespoons carrier oil, such as almond or jojoba
- 2 drops of ginger essential oil
- 2 drops of sandalwood essential oil
- 1 drop of bergamot essential oil
- 1 drop of patchouli essential oil
- 1 bay leaf
- 1 tablespoon cinnamon chips

Steps:

- Cleanse your altar.
- Pour the carrier oil into an amber roller bottle.
- Add the ginger, sandalwood, bergamot, and patchouli essential oils, one at a time. As you add each ingredient, chant the phrase *"Money, grow and multiply."*
- Add the bay leaf and cinnamon chips.
- Hold the bottle in your hands and envision energy wrapping around it. Charge it with your intentions.
- Gently shake the bottle before each use to ensure the elements are combined. Use the oil on your skin, charms, or other objects.

Growing Riches Spell

This spell uses Money Grow Dressing Oil and a mint plant, which you can buy at any grocery store that sells herbs. Mint is very useful for attracting money and has a variety of uses. A mint plant is a valuable investment for any witch.

When to Perform This Spell: During a new moon

Time to Allot for the Spell: 15 minutes

Where to Perform the Spell: Altar or kitchen

Ingredients/Tools:

- ❖ Mint plant
- ❖ 4 items that represent each of the four elements (e.g., a bowl of water, soil, a candle, and a besom)
- ❖ Coin or money charm
- ❖ Money Grow Dressing Oil

Steps:

- ❖ Cleanse your altar or kitchen space.

- ❖ Place your new mint plant on your altar and spend time consecrating it. To consecrate the mint plant, pass it through your four elements or ask the elements to assist with consecrating. Both methods utilize your desire to purify, charge, and bless. You can use words or think silently about your goals.
- ❖ When you are finished, anoint the coin or charm with Money Grow Dressing Oil to charge it for use. Place it near the base of the mint plant.
- ❖ Close your eyes and meditate on your intention for the mint plant to grow and attract money.
- ❖ You can pick the anointed mint leaves and carry them as a charm or use them in other money spells.

Money Knot Spell

This knot spell stores and binds your intention to attract money in every knot you tie. You can use any combination of money herbs as incense in this spell, including basil, bay leaf, chamomile, cinnamon, clove, dill, or ginger.

When to Perform This Spell: On a Thursday or during a full moon or waxing moon

Time to Allot for the Spell: 30 minutes

Where to Perform the Spell: Altar

Ingredients/Tools:

- Lighter or matches
- Money Powder or a powdered blend of any money herbs
- Charcoal disc
- Heat-proof dish
- 3 green tea light candles
- 1 (12-inch) piece of green, gold, or white string

Steps:

- Cleanse your altar.

- Burn the Money Powder on a charcoal disc on a heat-proof dish and arrange the tea light candles in a triangular configuration.
- Light the candles and focus on your intention of generating more money.
- Tie five knots in your string. As you tie each knot, say,

"With knot one, the spell has begun, with knot two, the spell will come true, with knot three, the spell hears my plea, with knot four, the spell grows more, with knot five, the spell is alive."

- Allow the tea light candles to continue burning while you meditate for 15 minutes, visualizing what you want to manifest.

133

Prosperity Talisman

This spell will consecrate and charge a piece of jewelry with your intentions of prosperity and wealth. This particular version uses a necklace, but you may alter it for any piece of jewelry, crystal, stone, or another pendant of choice. To amplify the spell, use a necklace made with crystal or wood. Wear it under your clothes, hidden from others.

When to Perform This Spell: On a Sunday or during a new moon

Time to Allot for the Spell: 15 minutes

Where to Perform the Spell: Altar

Ingredients/Tools:

- ❖ Necklace
- ❖ Pinch of dried mint
- ❖ White or green votive or pillar candle
- ❖ Lighter or matches

Steps:

- ❖ Cleanse your altar.
- ❖ Purify the necklace.

- ❖ Sprinkle the dried mint on the top of the candle.
- ❖ Light the candle and focus on visualizing its money properties.
- ❖ Move your necklace through the smoke and say,

"Necklace I charge with prosperity, attract to me riches and wealth, and serve me well with sincerity while you're worn in secret stealth."

- ❖ Allow some of your power to infuse the object, charging it for use.
- ❖ You may use the same candle to repeat the spell every few months.

Pay Stub Growth Spell

Bless and grow your pay stub. This may very well be the safest and least obtrusive path to using magic to increase your prosperity.

You will need:

- ❖ Your pay stubs
- ❖ A seedling
- ❖ Garden soil
- ❖ A small plant pots

Steps:

- ❖ Put the garden soil into the plant pot.

- ❖ Dig into the garden soil and "plant" your pay stub. As you do, recite the following: *"The fruit of my work, the seed which I plant. Grow seed grow. Your fruit is so sweet."*

- ❖ Plant the seedling on top of the pay stub.

- ❖ Nurture and care for this plant throughout the growing season.

Spell for Saving

Some people find saving to be a simple and obvious concept to put into practice, while others cannot hold onto that last dime in their pocket. How nice would it be if everyone was able to hoard their savings healthily? The first thing you will need to do is to go to a bank and open a savings account. Then, write a plan detailing how you will save (how frequently you will contribute; how much you will contribute; how you will make that happen, etc.). Remember that magick works **with** real-world action, not instead of it.

You will need:

- ❖ A few stones (anything found in nature that appeals to you)

- ❖ A brown cord

- ❖ A statement/printout from your savings account

Instructions:

- ❖ Cast a sacred circle. When you consecrate the elements, include the stones in the Earth consecration, by putting them in the salt dish

- ❖ Consecrate the cords by the four elements and recite the following:

"Air and Fire. Water and Earth. Consecrate this tool of magick that binds me to the commitment I make."

- ❖ Now consecrate the bank statement by the four elements, and say:

"Air and Fire. Water and Earth. Consecrate this tool of finance that holds and keeps the commitment I make."

- ❖ Stand within the sacred circle and rub them over your body, from head to toe. Feel yourself grounded and connected to Earth as you do so.

- ❖ Visualize trunks full of buried treasure, gold mines, and any other ways that Earth helps us hold, save, and store treasure.

- ❖ Hold the statement in your non-dominant hand. Use the cord to bind the statement to you. As you do so, recite the following:

"I am bound to save. So mote it be."

- ❖ Close the sacred circle.

Short Term Money Spell

Money is just one of those life necessities, whether we like it or not. It is simply a fact of life. Like any life necessity, a spell can easily aid in the process of acquiring what you need. This spell can assist you in gaining that quick infusion of money when you are going to be a bit short.

You will need:

- Cinnamon Incense
- A small bowl of sea or mineral salt
- A small bowl of moon water
- 1 Red Candle
- Dried Basil
- 1 Citrine crystal
- Fingernail or hair clippings
- A coin from the year of your birth (avoid pennies)
- A token that represents your work to you
- 1 green sachet
- A length of brown string

Instructions:

- Cast a protective circle.
- Light the red candle and begin to burn the incense.
- Ground and Center your energy.
- Meditation and visualization play key roles in the success of this spell. Meditate and visualize your life when the money you want is already with you. Let that sense of calm confidence wash over you. Focus on every detail that you visualize - how you feel after getting the money, how you spend the money, and what this money does for you in your life.
- Rinse the Citrine in flowing water. As you add ingredients to the sachet, pass the item through the incense

smoke, and then place the items in the bag.

* When all of the items have been added to the bag, tie the sachet closed with the length of brown string.

* Sprinkle the outside of the sachet with the salt.

* Spritz the outside of the sachet with the moon water.

* While holding the sachet in your dominant hand, recite the following:

"Money is the thing I need. The act is pure in heart and deed. I ask that you grant all to me. Smile your smile of gold. So mote it be."

* Allow the red candle to burn itself out.

* Close the sacred circle.

* Keep the sachet nearby (in a pocket, in a purse, in a briefcase, etc.)

Money Rain Spell with a Catholic Candle Prayer

Ingredients:

- ❖ Coarse salt

- ❖ A cup or your chalice

- ❖ 1 white candle

- ❖ 1 image or Prayer card to Saint Expedite

How to Cast the Spell:

- ❖ Make sure the salt is in the chalice or cup before putting it on your shrine.

- ❖ When you put the picture of St. Expedite in the cup, put some of it near the salt.

- ❖ The white candle is lit.

- ❖ This is what you should do: Cross your body and say the following prayer:

- ❖ Catholic-Money-Rain-Prayer

- ❖ Ensure you don't leave the room when you let the candle burn out.

- ❖ It's a good idea to keep the picture of Saint Expedite in your wallet with a pinch of salt next to it. Throw away the rest of the salt and the wax from the candle.

139

Prosperity Oil Recipe

Ingredients:

- ❖ Herbs (and their relevant qualities)

- ❖ Clean glass jar or bottle

- ❖ Jasmine – Money

- ❖ Cinnamon – Money, Speeds Up Spells

- ❖ Carrier oil e.g., Olive, Grapeseed

- ❖ Green glitter (optional)

- ❖ Patchouli – Prosperity

- ❖ Lavender – Prosperity, Protection

- ❖ Dragon's Blood – Purification, Protection, Amplifies Magical Workings

- ❖ Sage, Palo Santo or other Cleansing Incense

- ❖ Sandalwood Protection, Manifestation

How to Cast the Spell:

- ❖ Light some sage, Palo Santo, or other incense that is good for your body and mind.

"I ask that the plant spirit of Palo Santo please bless this space."

"With this smoke, I remove all negative or harmful energy from this object so that I can use it for my highest good," you say as you pick up the jar and fan it with the smoke.

- ❖ What was said, will happen.

- ❖ Take each ingredient and make it more powerful with your intentions.

- ❖ Add olive oil or another type of oil; shake everything together.

- ❖ It is important to use these sacred plants respectfully and thank them for their help when you do magic.

140

❖ Thank you, plant spirit, for your good fortune.

❖ You now have a great oil called Prosperity Oil.

Health and Wellness Spell Jar

To Heal the Body

This spell hones in on the malady or pain that is affecting your body, whether that malady is physical, emotional, or spiritual.

Ingredients:

- ❖ A large piece of paper
- ❖ Yellow, purple, and red felt-tipped pens
- ❖ A black marker pen

Ritual:

- ❖ The first thing that you are going to do is take your large piece of paper and draw three concentric circles on it.

- ❖ Use the felt-tipped pens to color the concentric circles. The inner-circle should be purple. The middle circle should be yellow and the outer one red.

- ❖ Now above the three concentric circles, add another circle. Below the concentric circles, draw two lines. This way, the concentric circles represent your body, the circle above indicates your head and the two lines below the concentric circles represent your legs.

- ❖ Now think of the pain that you are feeling. This could be physical, emotional, or spiritual pain. Take out your black marker and place a dot on the region that represents your pain. Here are what each of the regions in the concentric circles represents.

- ❖ Red represents physical pain

- ❖ Yellow represents the emotional distress or discomfort that you are enduring

- ❖ Purple focuses on spiritual maladies

- ❖ Once you know the regions, you can place a dot in the respective region, depending on the type of pain you are feeling. Each time you place a dot, speak these words:

Raphael, Raphael Angel of ease

Help me to understand this pain, please

❖ Now sit quietly and absorb the color that you have marked into your body. If you have marked all three colors, then absorb them one by one.

❖ When you have absorbed one color, visualize a white light entering your body as well. This white light is going to clear out the color from your body, in turn helping you deal with the problem.

❖ You have to perform this ritual for the next two days.

❖ At the end of those two days, you might be able to better understand the cause of the trauma.

NOTE: Remember that this ritual is not a replacement for actual medical diagnosis. Though it might bring about healing effects to your body, it does not get rid of the problem entirely. Make sure that you get medical attention wherever you see fit.

Good Health Wish

This is a simple spell that is best performed during the phase of the New Moon.

Ingredients:

- ❖ 3 bay leaves
- ❖ A piece of paper
- ❖ Pen

Ritual:

- ❖ During the New Moon, write down your wish for good health. Visualize what happens when the wish comes true. Imagine yourself enjoying life with a good spirit.

- ❖ Fold the paper into thirds, making sure that the bay leaves are placed inside.

- ❖ Bring the paper close to your heart and visualize the wish coming true again.

- ❖ One gain, fold the paper in thirds.

- ❖ Keep the paper in a dark place, such as a closet or a drawer.

- ❖ Every night, before you head to bed, visualize the wish coming true.

- ❖ When the wish does come true and you are in good health, burn the paper as a way of saying thanks.

Removing Negative Emotions

When you are overwhelmed by negative emotions, then you can make use of the rather simple spell to get rid of them.

Ingredients:

❖ A dark stone

Ritual:

❖ Lie down comfortably on the ground or floor. You can choose to be close to your altar or any other space that is comfortable for you.

❖ Close your eyes and imagine that there is a circle of white light surrounding you.

❖ Take the stone and place it above your solar plexus.

❖ Imagine that all your negative emotions are flowing into the stone. Imagine your anger, envy, deep-rooted resentments, and other emotions being absorbed by the stone.

❖ Try to focus on one emotion at a time. If the emotion is anger, then imagine a red energy exiting your body and getting absorbed by the stone. If it is envy, then imagine a yellow energy. This way, give a color to each of the negative emotions.

❖ Once you have transferred all of your negative energies into the stone, place it over your head so that you can gain clarity about these emotions or energies.

❖ Place the stone over your heart. Recite the verse below clearly:

With this stone

Negative be gone,

Let water cleanse it

Back where it belongs.

❖ Once you have recited the above verse, take the stone outside and bring it to a source of running water, such as a river or a stream. Toss the stone inside. You can also throw it out into the open sea or a lake.

❖ If no sources of water are near you, then you can hurl the stone as far away from you as possible.

Healing Depression

Never should you assume that spells can be a replacement for proper medical care. Depression is a serious condition and even though this spell can bring relief to you, it is not a permanent solution. I would still recommend that you consult with a doctor and find a solution that helps you in the long term.

Ingredients:

- A red pouch or a talisman bag
- If you are a man, then pick a piece of pine cone
- If you are a woman, then pick a piece of angelica root
- A sprig of rosemary
- White candle
- A lucky token or coin
- A dog tag
- Clary sage oil which you will use to dress the objects
- Clary sage incense
- A pin or a burin

Ritual:

- One of the best parts of this ritual is that you can perform it on yourself or for somebody else.
- If you or the person the ritual is focused on are male, then write down the name of the person on the pine cone.
- If you or the person the ritual is focused on are female, then write down the name of the person on the angelica root.
- When you have chosen the lucky token or coin, make sure that it is a representation of the person. In other words, it should be something that reminds you of the person. If you are focusing on yourself, then use an object that you feel links to you.
- Once you have the token in your hands, say the below line:

May this good luck token come with healing to [the individual's name].

- ❖ Now inscribe the name of the person (if it is yourself, then your name) on the dog tag. As you are writing down the name, go over the above words again.

- ❖ Set the items in a pouch

- ❖ Set some oil to the bag for dropping

- ❖ Now use the oil to anoint the token and dog tag, then place these items in the pouch or the bag. Seal the bag or pouch tightly.

- ❖ Light up the incense and keep the bag in the smoke.

- ❖ Light up the candle next and pass the bag over the flame of the candle.

- ❖ If you have performed the ritual for yourself, then keep the bag with you for at least a week. If you have performed the ritual for someone else, then present the bag to them and tell them to keep it with them or close to them for a minimum of 7 days.

Healing Candle Spell

What you'll need:

- ❖ A blue, white, or yellow candle

- ❖ Healing Oil: angelica, comfrey, and chamomile

- ❖ A small, thin paintbrush

- ❖ A dish or candleholder

- ❖ Matches

- ❖ Tibetan healing incense

- ❖ An incense holder

- ❖ A small knife, or screw

Steps:

- ❖ Cast your circle and anoint the candle. With the small knife or screw tip, carve the words "heal me" on both sides of the candle, then light the candle. Light the incense and allow the smoke to drift across the candle flame, filling the room with a healing scent. (Place the incense far enough away from you so that you are not directly breathing the line of smoke).

- ❖ Allow your mind to drift into an alpha state: your gaze is out of focus, your mind is calm, and thoughts are discarded as they enter the space of your mind. As the candle burns, know that you are in the right place for healing of the spirit, mind, body, and soul. Feel the benevolent energy fill your circle. Feel the power of the universe filling your circle with healing light.

- ❖ When you are ready, open the circle and ground. Allow the candle and incense to burn down.

Conjuring Relief from Anxiety and Depression

This spell can be used for either anxiety, which boils down to a fear of the future, or depression, which often indicates being stuck in the regrets of the past. The ritual is the same for either, though the signifying colors of the candle are distinct.

When to Perform: Any time during the waning moon

How Long It Takes: As long as it takes the candles to burn down for nine days

What You'll Need:

- ❖ 1 white pillar candle for anxiety OR
- ❖ 1 red pillar candle for depression
- ❖ Orange essential oil
- ❖ Crystal or stone (optional)

Steps:

- ❖ Smudge your space well: you want your energy to be clear and fresh.

- ❖ Place your candle in the center of the altar and anoint it with orange essential oil. This replaces anxiety or depression with strength and vitality. The white candle is to purify your mind of anxiety, while the red candle fortifies you with courage.

- ❖ Light the candle and, if you like, choose a particular crystal or stone to pass through the flame, drawing symbolic energy to you (a moonstone for peace, perhaps, or a bloodstone for courage). As the candle burns, recite your incantation:

"My power of self is so clearly strong, that no worries or troubles can come along. I cast protection against these worries in my soul because might is my weapon and harmony is my goal."

- ❖ Let the candle burn for a few minutes as you meditate on peacefulness and strength, then snuff it. Repeat this ritual each

day at the same time for
nine consecutive days.

Planting Happiness Spell

Happiness is often just within reach, but not quite within our grasp. Cast this spell to radiate happiness that will leave you glowing and feeling in sync with the moment. In this spell, you'll plant a tree or shrub, which will allow you to find happiness in nature.

When to Perform This Spell: On a Wednesday or Sunday

Time to Allot for the Spell: 45 minutes

Where to Perform the Spell: Outdoors

Ingredients/Tools:

- ❖ Shielding Mist (optional)
- ❖ Shovel
- ❖ Plant or tree
- ❖ 5 clear quartz crystals
- ❖ Gardening gloves (optional)
- ❖ Shovel
- ❖ Water (enough to water your plant—the amount varies from plant to plant, so do your research!)
- ❖ Dash salt

Steps:

- ❖ Use your intuition to choose an outdoor spot (e.g., somewhere in your garden) for your happiness plant or tree.
- ❖ Cleanse the chosen area. If you'd like to, spray it with Shielding Mist.
- ❖ Use the tip of the shovel to scratch out a pentagram shape in the earth that encompasses you and your plant.
- ❖ Place the clear quartz crystals at the points of the pentagram.
- ❖ Begin digging a hole in the soil. Wear gardening gloves if you'd like.
- ❖ Place your plant or tree in the hole. Pack dirt up to the base of the plant to stabilize it.
- ❖ Spend 10 minutes meditating silently next to the plant, reaching out with your consciousness to

connect with its energy.
While meditating, say,

"Plant of happiness, fill my life,

brighten my heart, and lift my spirit."

- ❖ Water your plant and sprinkle the salt as an offering in the surrounding area.
- ❖ Care for your plant weekly, repeating your meditation and chant.

Well-Being Anointing Oil

In this spell, you'll blend, charge, and bless this magical anointing oil. Use this oil on objects, in well-being spells, or on your pulse points as a way to amplify your intentions to attract positivity into your life. If applying to your skin, remember to do a patch test.

When to Perform This Spell: During a new or full moon

Time to Allot for the Spell: 20 minutes

Where to Perform the Spell: Altar or kitchen

Ingredients/Tools:

- ❖ Small amber roller bottle or dropper bottle
- ❖ 1 tablespoon carrier oil, such as jojoba or almond oil
- ❖ 2 drops patchouli essential oil
- ❖ 2 drops of lavender essential oil
- ❖ 2 drops of ylang-ylang essential oil
- ❖ 1 teaspoon dried chamomile

Steps:

- ❖ Cleanse your altar.
- ❖ Add the carrier oil to an amber roller bottle.
- ❖ Next, add in the patchouli, lavender, and ylang-ylang essential oils while focusing on your intentions.
- ❖ Add the chamomile to fill any empty space.
- ❖ Hold the bottle in your hands and envision energy wrapping around it. Charge it with your intentions. Say,

"With this oil, I blend and bless,

well-being and feelings of gratefulness."

- ❖ Wear it whenever you need to live in the moment and attract positivity

Ritual for Banishment of Internal Darkness

You will need:

- ❖ A clear glass bottle

- ❖ A small piece of clear quartz

- ❖ Enough spring water to fill the glass bottle

- ❖ A few drops of peppermint essential oil

- ❖ A few drops of lemon essential oil

- ❖ A few drops of sweet orange essential oil

- ❖ Strength card from an unused Tarot deck

Instructions:

- ❖ Cast a sacred circle.

- ❖ Fill the bottle with the spring water, add the drops of essential oils, and lastly add the clear quartz.

- ❖ Cap the bottle.

- ❖ Shake the bottle three times to mix and charge the elixir.

- ❖ Place the bottle on the face-up Strength card and allow it to sit undisturbed for at least 10 minutes.

- ❖ Open the bottle and remove the crystal.

- ❖ Drink the elixir. As you drink, visualize the charged liquid entering your body and spreading from your stomach out; engulfing and transforming any pockets of darkness into radiant light.

❖ Close the sacred circle.

Mental Wellness Spell

You will need:

 ❖ Soothing music (new age, classical, chants)

 ❖ A tumbled amethyst

 ❖ A tumbled rose quartz

 ❖ A blue candle with a candle holder

 ❖ Lavender essential oil

 ❖ Vanilla essential oil

 ❖ Sweet orange essential oil

Instructions:

 ❖ Center and ground your energy.

 ❖ Begin to play your selected music.

 ❖ Dress the blue candle with the essential oils.

 ❖ Cast a sacred circle.

 ❖ Light the dressed candle.

 ❖ Sit in the center of the circle, holding one of the crystals in each hand. Close your eyes.

 ❖ Breath slowly and deeply. Inhale the scents from around you and allow them to calm and soothe your mind.

 ❖ Rub the smooth crystals with your fingers.

 ❖ Focus on your breathing. When your mind begins to wander, bring it back to focus with the word, "Peace."

 ❖ When you begin to feel calm and your mind has quieted down, open your eyes, and snuff the candle.

❖ Close the sacred circle.

Peace Spell

This spell will create harmony between people. Use this spell when you want to stop arguments before they start.

Ingredients:

- ❖ 2 tablespoons of cinnamon powder
- ❖ 2 tablespoons of clove powder
- ❖ 2 teaspoons of ginger powder
- ❖ 2 tablespoons each of allspice and nutmeg
- ❖ 3 cups of water

Instructions:

- ❖ Blend together thoroughly.
- ❖ *Say these words:*

"I ask that you send peace to everyone who has ever wronged me. I ask that you bring peace to my troubled soul. Thank you for listening to my prayers."

- ❖ Visualize your intention while blending the ingredients. Then, add 10 drops of jasmine essential oil.

- ❖ Strain the mixture through a cheesecloth.

- ❖ Pour the liquid into a bowl and add 10 drops of patchouli essential oil. Visualize your intention while stirring the mixture.

- ❖ Allow the mixture to sit overnight.

- ❖ The following day, pour the mixture into a bottle. Cap the bottle and keep it away from sunlight and heat. Shake the bottle daily for one week.

Strength Spell

This spell will enhance your physical strength. Use this spell if it feels like you are lacking in physical strength.

Ingredients:

- ❖ 4 tablespoons of turmeric powder

- ❖ 1 tablespoon each of fennel seed

- ❖ Cinnamon

- ❖ Ginger

- ❖ Cloves

- ❖ Cardamom

- ❖ Black peppercorns

- ❖ Coriander seeds

Instructions:

- ❖ Say these words:

"Goddess, please strengthen my body. Give me energy whenever I need it."

- ❖ Put the spices into a small saucepan and cover them with water. Bring the mixture to a boil. Reduce the heat to low and simmer for 30 minutes. Strain the mixture through a cheesecloth.

- ❖ Pour the strained mixture into a bottle. Add 10 drops of eucalyptus essential oil. Cap the bottle and place it in a cool, dark area. Shake the bottle daily.

Blocking Illness: A Protection Spell

Most people who practice magic acquire a repertoire of healing and protective tools, including amulets, sachets, potions, and spells. Herbs, in particular, are key to most healing rituals and can be used in a variety of combinations for a myriad of results. Here is a general health spell using candles: you can amplify its power or specify its intentions with the addition of particular herbal oils or dried herbs, depending on your needs.

When to Perform: During a full moon

How Long It Takes: As long as it takes the candles to burn down

What You'll Need:

- ❖ 1 white taper candle
- ❖ 1 indigo taper candle
- ❖ 1 purple taper candle

Steps:

- ❖ Smudge your space with a mix of sage and rosemary for maximum protection and cleansing.

- ❖ Arrange your candles in a triangle with the white "self" candle at the apex. The indigo represents physical health, while the purple candle symbolizes spiritual well-being.

- ❖ Call upon each of the elements to aid in protection:

"I call upon the earth to keep me grounded. I call upon the fire to purge me of fever. I call upon the water to wash away infection. I call upon the wind to whisk away bad energies."

- ❖ Let the candles burn all the way down, and when the wax remnants are cool, keep them under your pillow until the next full moon, then bury them beneath a strong and sturdy tree.

Rapid Recovery: A Spell for Quick Healing

This spell is appropriate for a particular wound or illness. While the previous spell is, at its core, a protection spell, this is a more focused conjuring. It may not be powerful enough to heal chronic conditions, but I have used it to good effect when dealing with sprained ankles and head colds.

When to Perform: Any time it's needed

How Long It Takes: As long as it takes the candle to burn down

What You'll Need:

- ❖ 1 white taper candle
- ❖ Eucalyptus essential oil
- ❖ Black cord or string

Steps:

- ❖ Cleanse your space and set your candle at the center of your altar.

- ❖ Anoint the candle with the healing and cleansing eucalyptus oil. Use the cord or string to tie around the injured or ill part of the body, as close to the area as you can.

- ❖ Light the candle and state your intention: *"Close this wound, end the sick, make me healthy, sure, and quick."*

- ❖ Let the candle burn down, untying the cord and letting it burn—use caution. In the last moments of the dying flame, imagine the injury or illness being consumed by the flame. Be sure to get rid of remnants directly, sending them far away.

Hearty and Hale: A Spell to Improve Health

This spell uses candle magic in a slightly different way: you are focusing your magic on your homemade incense blend, using the candle to release the scents and energies into the atmosphere. This incense blend can also be brewed into a tea, assuming that you've used kitchen-grade products safe for consumption.

When to Perform: During a full moon

How Long It Takes: A couple of hours (mostly inactive)

What You'll Need:

- ❖ Incense Ingredients: dried orange peel, caraway seeds, black peppercorns, dried sage, rosemary, cinnamon, and natural sugar (such as demerara)
- ❖ 1 orange or red tea candle
- ❖ Flameproof incense burner or another vessel

Steps:

- ❖ This is best prepared in the kitchen, so smudge the kitchen with a strong sage bundle.

- ❖ Prepare your incense mixture by combining 1 tablespoon each of dried orange peel for vitality, caraway seeds for antiseptic properties, black peppercorns for endurance, sage for mental strength, rosemary for memory, cinnamon for physical strength, and sugar for sweetness (of life).

- ❖ Put your ingredients in an incense burner or other flameproof container and light your tea candle underneath the incense, releasing its scents and intentions into the room.

163

❖ Let it burn until it's
   spent, then bury the
   remnants in a place
   where healthy
   plants grow.

Spiritual Bath Spell for Good Luck

Ingredients:

- ❖ 1 white candle
- ❖ 1 sprig of Rue
- ❖ 3 leaves of Guinea hen weed
- ❖ 1 sprig of Rosemary

Why this Bath Works

- ❖ Rue is one of the most powerful herbs for spiritual healing because it has been used for a long time to protect people from psychic attacks, jealousy, curses, and more. Rue has been used this way for a long time. It is also very popular when cutting binds in love because Magic works that way. A rue bath makes you feel happy and rich.

- ❖ Rosemary is a traditional kitchen witchcraft herb that can remove negative energies from food, water, the body and the home. It helps to start healing processes that deal with self-love, beauty, desire, and more.

- ❖ Guinea Hen Weed grows in the Amazon rainforest and the Caribbean. It comes from Guinea Hen Weed. Shamans have used it for a long time to treat fevers anxiety and boost the immune system. This plant is made up of many antioxidants that fight infections and help with pain, so it's unique.

165

Road Opener Wiccan Candle Ritual

Ingredients:

❖ 1 white candle

❖ Bowl of water (regular drinking water)

❖ 1 incense stick

❖ 1 crystal or gemstone (pick 1 according to the day)

How to Cast the Spell:

❖ Make sure your items are on the altar in the correct order before you do this. They'll all face one of the four ways: Western-facing water Air faces East. Earth is facing north. Fire is facing South.

❖ A candle should be lit to make the incense smell. The Air element has come into your ritual.

❖ You want to rub your hands together for a few seconds until you feel warm energy. Then, visualize a ball of energy and hold your crystal. You are invoking the Earth element.

❖ Light the candle so that you can call on the Fire element to come to you.

❖ Gentle dip your finger in the water to feel like you're with the Water element. Water is like a mirror that can show you a different world. This transforming energy will remove all of the blocks.

❖ Chant the following prayer to open the road: A prayer chant to open the road

❖ An empty road comes to mind. As you see yourself moving forward, take a few minutes to think about where you want to go.

❖ Take care of the candle at all times. If you have to leave the room, you can put out the candle and keep it going when you get back.

❖ Toss the rest away once the candle has burned out and say "thank you." You should keep the crystal close to you to see it better. To use this spell's power, rub your hands together and hold it in your hands again.

'Bad Luck, Go Away!' Candle Spell to Remove a Curse

Ingredients:

- ❖ Salt

- ❖ 1 green candle

- ❖ Cinnamon powder

How to Cast the Spell:

- ❖ You can put the green candle on your shrine.

- ❖ Spread some salt around it to make a circle that protects it. Say: good-luck-spell-incantation

- ❖ The green candle is lit. Think about all the bad luck you've had. Say: go-away-bad-luck

- ❖ Imagine that all the problems in your life are gone.

- ❖ As soon as it has cooled down for 5 minutes, sprinkle the cinnamon powder over the salt.

- ❖ It helps to think of that extra good luck as a bright light that comes to you as you picture all the good things you want to happen in your life. Negative thoughts and memories should be erased and replaced with images of new chances.

- ❖ Burn it all the way through.

Good Luck & Prosperity Cinnamon Spell

Ingredients:

❖ Cinnamon incense

❖ Wooden incense holder

How to Cast the Spell:

❖ Place the cinnamon incense stick on the wooden incense holder and light it. This will help you to smell better.

❖ As many times as you want, say the following chant:

❖ It's good luck. Prosperity Chant is a spell.

❖ Take a deep breath and let the smoke from the cinnamon fill your home as you think about how it will clean and protect you from bad luck.

Magick Sun Sigil

Ingredients:

- ❖ Piece of paper
- ❖ 1 yellow candle
- ❖ Pen or pencil
- ❖ 1 incense stick or essential oil (such as Lemon, Lavender, Jasmine, Rosemary, Cinnamon, Peppermint).
- ❖ Your study books or course material

How to Cast the Spell:

- ❖ Make sure the incense is lit and take three deep breaths before you do anything else. Relax and have a good attitude. To ground yourself, you can make a circle or just sit still for a short time.
- ❖ Take a piece of paper and draw a picture of the sun. In any way you want, or keep it simple: It doesn't have to be very big to work. You need to put the sun sigil on something to pass a test.
- ❖ Light the yellow candle and say the spell: Using Spell to help me pass my test
- ❖ See yourself, or the Sun's spiritual power, coming to help you. Giving you the strength, focus, and memory, you need to do well on the test. Imagining the sun giving off its light will help you clear your mind so you can pass the exam.
- ❖ People can meditate for a few minutes or pray to a solar deity when they have some time on their hands. Find a list of guided pagan prayers here.
- ❖ Put out the candle when you're ready. You can blow it out. Keep the drawing with you. In the test, it will be your lucky amulet.

171

Charge & Activate Talismans or Amulets

Ingredients:

- ❖ 1 small bowl of salt
- ❖ 1 white candle
- ❖ 1 glass of water (or your chalice)
- ❖ 1 incense stick (pick any aroma that speaks to you)

How to Cast the Spell:

- ❖ There is a candle and some incense that needs to be lit,
- ❖ Stand facing North with the amulet in your hands.
- ❖ Hold it over the salt and say the chant:
- ❖ Amulet of blessing
- ❖ Turn to the East and, while holding the amulet over the smoke from the incense, say:

Consecrate an amulet.

- ❖ When you turn to the South, hold the amulet over the flame of a candle, be careful not to burn it.
- ❖ Finally, turn to the West, and hold your amulet over the water in the glass. Consecration of a water amulet:
- ❖ As you hold the amulet aloft, say Amulet blessing. Out loud, say what your amulet is for.
- ❖ Do not take off your amulet for the next five days.

Good Luck Spell Chant: Janus' New Beginnings

Ingredients:

- ❖ An old key
- ❖ 1 green candle
- ❖ Piece of paper
- ❖ 1 black candle
- ❖ Pen or pencil

How to Cast the Spell:

- ❖ Light the black candle and let it take in any negative thoughts you have about starting this new cycle, and then let them go away.

- ❖ The green candle is lit. Take a deep breath and think about your goal for the ritual.

- ❖ Use the pen to write down your goal on the paper. Do not be afraid to be as detailed as you need to be. You can write one word or a whole page of your thoughts.

- ❖ Use your pen or pencil to outline the key on the paper. If you don't have a key, you can copy this one from Roman history. The key is a symbol of unlocking the doors of change. The Janus Key

- ❖ Say this chant:

It's good luck. Spell out the words for Chant.

- ❖ Some green candle wax should be poured on the picture of the key.

- ❖ Meditate. Ensure the candle doesn't get too hot during the next few days. Make sure to keep the page in your book of mirrors. Check back with it in about three months to see if you've achieved your goal.

173

Good Luck Spell to Ward Off Negative Energies

Ingredients:

- ❖ 1 photo of yourself
- ❖ 1 large onion
- ❖ 1 white candle
- ❖ 1 glass of water
- ❖ Coarse salt (sea salt, Epsom salt, or other)

Why this Spell Works

Sea salt is a great purifying and protective agent. In ancient times, it was used to sterilize and keep food fresh. Because of this, spiritual traditions from all over the world believe that salt can be used to clean, bring good luck, and protect people. For this spell, you could use other types of salt, like Epsom salt or pink salt. You could also use other types of salt. Onions are said to keep bad things away. Traditionally, they were used to give warriors strength and courage and keep them healthy. Onion has been used for a long time in a lot of different spells for health, work, and divination.

A white candle symbolizes purity, God, and immaculate. Candles made of white wax are often used in rituals to make spaces more harmonious and positive and purify and clean them. They protect the home and bring peace to the soul.

Attract More Good Luck in the New Moon

Ingredients:

- ❖ Dish
- ❖ Coarse salt
- ❖ 1 white candle
- ❖ 7 red rose petals (dried or fresh)

How to Cast the Spell:

- ❖ The dish should be on your altar, so put it there. Use a handful of salt to make a circle around the dish to protect it.

- ❖ Place seven petals of a red rose on top of the salt circle.

- ❖ Light a white candle in the middle of the dish.

- ❖ Sit down, breathe slowly, and let go. All the paths in your life should become clear, and all the doors should open for you.

- ❖ This chant is for when you're ready: People who are grateful for help the moon can cast spells.

- ❖ Do the same thing with the same ingredients and candle for seven days. On the last day, let it go.

Protection Spells

Hex-Reversal Mirror Spell - To Break a Curse

Ingredients:

- ❖ 1 mirror
- ❖ Waning Moon

How to Cast the Spell:

- ❖ Find a medium-sized oval-shaped mirror and make sure it is clean and not broken before using it.

- ❖ On the back of the mirror, write:

- ❖ spell to reverse the direction of the candle

- ❖ Make a circle on the ground when the Moon is going down. You can bring your favorite tool and make a circle if you want to.

- ❖ It's best to place it inside a circle, with its mirror-side facing up. A chant for hex reversal:

- ❖ The mirror has been made holy and is now there to protect you from bad things. Outside by the door or inside your house (facing outwards).

176

Cord-Cutting Spell

Ingredients:

- ❖ 1 white candle
- ❖ Lighter or matches
- ❖ Your Athame or Wand

How to Cast the Spell:

- ❖ In front of you, light the white candle.

- ❖ Relax and keep your eyes on your breath. Close your eyes and let your mind drift off.

- ❖ Let the places where things connect come to you. Let the cords show up. They should look like laces that connect you to that person. No, they aren't. To heart? Do not judge where the cords are because they could be in places you didn't expect. Each cord could be different. There is a chance that they are taking energy from you or giving you different kinds of feelings. Think about them for a minute.

- ❖ Open your eyes and stand up slowly. It's best to hold your weapon in your dominant hand if you have a wand or athame. If you don't have one, you can use your finger. Stretch your arm out in front of you. When you turn your body to the right, do it slowly. Keep turning until you've made a full circle.

- ❖ These affirmations can be said out loud or said in your head.

- ❖ Switch sides as you do this, picturing how each cord is cut to the bone. Every time you cut one, a protective circle of healing light

surrounds   you,
making your wound
better.

Candle Spell to Remove a Curse

Ingredients:

- ❖ Salt
- ❖ 1 green candle
- ❖ Cinnamon powder

How to Cast the Spell:

- ❖ You can put the green candle on your shrine.

- ❖ Spread some salt around it to make a circle that protects it. Say: good-luck-spell-incantation

- ❖ The green candle is lit. Think about all the bad luck you've had. Say: go-away-bad-luck

- ❖ Imagine that all the problems in your life are gone.

- ❖ As soon as it has cooled down for 5 minutes, sprinkle the cinnamon powder over the salt.

- ❖ It helps to think of that extra good luck as a bright light that comes to you as you picture all the good things you want to happen in your life. Negative thoughts and memories should be erased and replaced with images of new chances.

- ❖ Burn it all the way through.

179

Hyssop Charm':
Magic Anti-Stress
Tea Spell

Ingredients:

- ❖ Water

- ❖ 1 mug or teacup

- ❖ Hyssop tea (1 tea bag or 1 tablespoon of loose leaves)

- ❖ 1 blue candle (optional)

How to Cast the Spell:

- ❖ When the water starts to boil, heat it.

- ❖ While that's happening, turn off all phones or turn off notifications. Breathe deeply and let go.

- ❖ Add the hyssop tea to your cup, and then add the water and stir it in well.

- ❖ If you have a blue candle, light it.

- ❖ Relax. Use the guided meditation

video on this page as you slowly drink from your teacup, and take your time.

Spell to Stop Bullying

Ingredients:

- ❖ Screwcap bottle (e.g., an old pickle jar)

- ❖ 2 tablespoon Vinegar (any kind: brown, white wine, red or cider)

- ❖ Dried Mint

How to Cast the Spell:

- ❖ You can hold the glass jar in your hands. Picture the person leaving you alone and doing no harm to you in your mind.

- ❖ "(Person's name), you will not bully and intimidate me anymore!" say out loud.

- ❖ Some dried mint should also be added.

- ❖ Keep shaking your jar very hard as you say this spell nine times:

"Venom, viciousness, and vilest be gone!"

- ❖ Get out the lid. Pour what's inside down the drain while the hot water comes out of the faucet. Think about all the bad things that go down the drain with it.

- ❖ "It's time to wash this bottle." "Your power over me has been lost. I'm not going to get hurt. I am no longer bothered by you, and I'm free now that we're no longer together. Do not bother me anymore."

- ❖ Toss the bottle. Keep it clean if you want to. Do not let this energy get into your next spell for this jar.

181

Protecting Home and Hearth

This spell is ideal for when you first move into a new living space: you can ensure that any negative energy put out by previous occupants is dispelled, and reassure your own sense of safety. To fortify, recast the spell each year on the anniversary of your initial move-in.

When to Perform it:
When needed

How Long It Takes: 2 days

What You'll Need:

- ❖ 1 black taper candle

- ❖ 1white taper candle

- ❖ Lemon and rose essential oils

- ❖ 4 small glass jars

- ❖ Dried lavender, basil, salt and rice

Steps:

- ❖ The day before you intend to cast the spell, thoroughly smudge your entire house. Get up at sunrise (an auspicious time) and tidy everything before doing a sage smudging.

- ❖ Fill each of your jars with lavender, basil, salt, and rice, respectively, and place them in the four cardinal directions in your home—on a windowsill, if possible—or out in the garden, if you have one. The lavender brings peacefulness to the household, while the basil offers protection; the salt wards-off negative energies, while the rice is thought to bring good fortune. Let the moonlight charge these containers overnight.

- ❖ The next day, preferably at sunrise, arrange your jars in the four cardinal directions on your altar with the candles in between. Light your black candle to banish evil, your white candle to purify. Anoint the black candle with lemon essential oil for protection, your white candle with rose oil for blessings.

❖ Cast your spell with clear intentions:

"Bless this house, with peace and love. Cleanse all that should be rid of. Protect all those dwelling here, to keep us close, safe, and dear."

❖ Let the candles burn down entirely, and bury the wax remnants near your foundation. You can keep the jars on your window sills for a few weeks if you like, and/or you can use the contents to conjure up some magically enhanced potions and meals. Some practitioners don't use the herbs or other edible ingredients that have been a part of their spells, but I find it perfectly acceptable, not only because it infuses some magic into what I eat, but also because it keeps with the spirit of economy and recycling that is a part of any good spellcaster's philosophy.

183

Safe Voyages: A Protection Spell for Travel

This is a quick and easy spell that you can perform whenever you're going on a trip.

When to Perform: When needed: best on Wednesday before you embark on your journey

How Long It Takes: As long as it takes the candle to burn down

What You'll Need:

- ❖ 1 white taper candle
- ❖ Rosemary essential oil
- ❖ Rose quartz crystal

Steps:

- ❖ Consider smudging your entire house, rather than just your altar for this spell. This will also banish negative energies in your home, keeping everything positive for your return.

- ❖ Anoint your candle and the crystal with the protective rosemary oil, light the candle, and cast your spell:

"I call upon the spirit of the moon, to help me reach my destination soon. I want my trip happy and safe to be, for all involved, including me." Pass the crystal through the flame three times while you repeat your incantation.

- ❖ Carry the crystal with you on your journey. Store the remnants of the candle somewhere safe until you return, then bury them close to your home.

Avoiding Accidents: A Prevention Spell

Essentially, this spell teaches you how to make a talisman that you can carry with you for general safety. I keep this pouch of ingredients in my car and thus far it's worked like a literal charm!

When to Perform: During a full moon

How Long It Takes: As long as it takes for the candle to burn

What You'll Need:

- ❖ 1 black taper candle
- ❖ Small pouch
- ❖ Dried sage, rosemary, and salt
- ❖ Amethyst crystal
- ❖ Personal item (see steps below)

Steps:

- ❖ Cleanse your altar before you begin, and if you have the time, charge the crystal in the moonlight before you cast your spell.

- ❖ Place your candle in the center of your space, and light it while reciting your incantation:

"Here I ask that safe I'll be, no matter how wild and free. Use these things to protect me from harm, infuse them with power to work like a charm."

- ❖ As you let your candle burn, fill the pouch with your ingredients: a teaspoon or two of each of your protection herbs, along with the salt; add the amethyst crystal for soothing fear, and put in a personal item that you feel has magical properties to you. For example, I use whiskers from my cats (not pulled out, of course. I collect them as they are shed). But you can use anything you feel is a personal good luck charm.

- ❖ Keep the talismanic pouch in your car or your purse or briefcase so that it watches over you at all times.

Legal Relief: A Spell to Win a Court Case

As anyone knows who has ever faced any kind of legal snafu, this can take a toll on your peace of mind (not to mention your time and energy). This spell can help you "sweeten the deal," as it were, and bring positive results to any kind of court case you find yourself negotiating.

When to Perform: Seven days before the court date

How Long It Takes: As long as it takes for the candle to burn

What You'll Need:

- 1 brown tea candle
- Small jar
- Honey
- Black mustard seeds, cayenne pepper, and galangal root
- Pen and paper (optional)

Steps:

- Cleanse your space before you begin. You can put this together in your kitchen, if you like, after a good sage smudging.

- Pour the honey into the jar, and add a tablespoon of black mustard seeds to confuse your opponents, a couple of pinches of cayenne pepper to ward off negative energy, and three slices of fresh galangal root (or a couple of teaspoons powdered) for good luck and protection.

- Light your brown tea candle and recite your incantation:

"Keep me grounded and help me win, vanquish my enemies and save my skin!" Let the candle burn all the way down, then place the remnants in your spell jar and keep it in an auspicious place until the results are in.

187

Conjuring Peace: A Spell for a Happy Household

This spell attracts the positive energies needed to keep everyone in your home getting along with one another. The spell jar is intended to sit at a central place in your home, where it will draw on all the fundamental elements to keep the positive energy flowing.

When to Perform: Any time during a waxing moon, though a Friday is thought to be best

How Long It Takes: As long as it takes for the candles to burn

What You'll Need:

- ❖ 2 blue tea candles - 2 yellow tea candles
- ❖ Vanilla essential oil
- ❖ Small glass jar
- ❖ Dried basil, lavender, thyme, catnip, and lemon peel
- ❖ Lapis lazuli stone - Rose quartz stone
- ❖ A couple of drops of sun-charged water

Steps:

- ❖ Cleanse your altar space, as per usual, and prepare your spell jar. Add a tablespoon each of basil for protection and luck, lavender for peace, thyme for joy, catnip for attraction, and lemon peel for happiness.

- ❖ Anoint the stones with a couple of drops of sun-charged water (water that has been exposed to full sunlight for three hours), then place them in the jar: the lapis lazuli soothes and invites intuition, while the rose quartz promotes friendship and romantic love.

- ❖ Place your candles in the four cardinal directions—the blue at north/earth and west/water, the yellow at south/fire and east/air—and anoint them with soothing vanilla essential oil.

- ❖ As you light the candles, cast your spell:

"Here I ask for this home to have peace, for all negative energy and strife to cease. I invite much happiness and joy to all who dwell here, girl and boy."

❖ Let the candles burn down, and bury their remains at the foundation of your home.

Vanquishing Visitors: A Spell to Get Rid of Unwanted Guests

We all know what it's like to have the obtuse guest who doesn't realize it's time to leave, whether that be an annoying uncle at the holidays or an old friend who's crashing on your couch. Here's a simple, but gentle, banishment spell to restore your privacy.

When to Perform: When needed

How Long It Takes: As long as it takes for the candle to burn

What You'll Need:

- ❖ 1 black taper candle
- ❖ Lemon or mint essential oil
- ❖ Black pepper, cayenne, and cinnamon

Steps:

- ❖ Cleanse your altar or space. You might consider smudging the area in which the unwanted guest has been sleeping (if you can do so while they aren't around).
- ❖ Anoint your black banishment candle with lemon or mint oil; both provide purification and protection for your space. Mix together your spices, about a tablespoon of each, and roll your candle in them: black pepper provides stamina and courage; cayenne sends away negative energy, and cinnamon brings protection.
- ❖ Light your candle and recite your incantation:

"Hear me now as I ask my guest to go, give me peace and end this woe." Repeat this seven times as you watch the candle burn.

- ❖ Be sure to get rid of the remnants as soon as possible: this might be an occasion for a handy toilet flush!

190

Under Your Thumb No More: A Spell to Free Yourself from Influence

If you've ever been involved in an unhealthy relationship, whether a romantic relationship or friendship went sour, or even a domineering family member, this spell can help you free yourself from that negative influence. You might also try casting a decision-making spell, as well, or a confidence spell to get you back to your own clarity of thinking.

When to Perform: Any time during a waning moon

How Long It Takes: As long as it takes to burn and scatter ashes

What You'll Need:

- ❖ 2 white taper candles
- ❖ 1 red or purple taper candle
- ❖ Pen and paper
- ❖ Flameproof bowl or dish

Steps:

- ❖ Cleanse your altar space, as per usual, and line up your candles with the red or purple candle in between your white candles. Choose red if the person of influence has controlled you with passion or anger; choose purple if that influence has been more psychological or spiritual. The white candles will pull that energy from the central candle, purifying your intentions.

- ❖ Write the person's name on the piece of paper and set it alight while you cast your spell:

"I ask that you step away from my life, freeing me from this constant strife. I reclaim my mind and soul, rejecting your influence and becoming whole."

- ❖ When your candles and paper have burned, scatter the ashes to the winds, bury the remnants of the white candles somewhere that brings you joy, and send the red or purple candle away in the water.

191

Karmic Returns: A Spell to Reverse Evil Sent to You

One of the most fundamental tenets of working magic is that you never wish harm to others. If you do, that karmic energy will return to you threefold. If you suspect someone has been engaging in this kind of magic against you, then you can return it to them—and let them rue the day they expelled that negative nonsense!

When to Perform: Start or end at the full moon

How Long It Takes: About 10 minutes a day for nine days

What You'll Need:

- ❖ 1 black pillar candle
- ❖ 1 white pillar candle
- ❖ 1 red pillar candle
- ❖ Cinnamon essential oil
- ❖ Penknife

Steps:

- ❖ Cleanse your space well; this spell requires a lot of power behind it.

- ❖ Prepare your candles: pick out some runes to carve into each candle. A pentacle is a banishing rune, which can work, or the algiz for protection in general (when rendered upside down, this rune also constitutes a warning), or the eihwaz for defense. Depictions of all of these can be found online. Alternately, you can carve your own symbology onto the candles, according to what works best for you. This can be as simple as carving your name into the white candle, your opponent's name into the black candle, and the offending deed into the red candle.

- ❖ Arrange your candles in a triangle, with the white candle at the apex and anoint with cinnamon oil, which brings both energy and protection to your spell.

- ❖ Cast your spell:

"I send back evil your way, three times three. Your bad intentions won't stay with me, as I return them to you, three times three."

192

Recite the incantation three times, then snuff the candles.

- ❖ Repeat the spell each day (ideally at the same time) for nine days.

Sleep Spell Jar

Divining Dreams: A Spell for Good Sleep

This spell should help you get a solid night's sleep. If you want to invite dreams, then add a stick of frankincense or lavender incense to burn during the spell.

When to Perform: Anytime you need deep sleep

How Long It Takes: As long as it takes the candle to burn down

What You'll Need:

- 1 blue tea candle
- Amethyst or smoke quartz crystal

Steps:

- Perform this spell directly in your bedroom, and prepare yourself and the room for good sleep. Obviously, you want to cleanse the space thoroughly, as usual, but you also want to invest in some more practical aids for good sleep. Put fresh, clean sheets on your bed, have a comfy blanket and your favorite pillow handy, turn off screens and keep the lighting dim, and consider playing some sleep-inducing music.

- When you are ready for bed, light your candle first and recite your incantation, with your crystal in your hand. The crystal is representative of the moon itself, inviting nighttime serenity. State your intentions clearly:

"Here in my hand, I hold the moon, so its calming light will soothe me soon."

- Let your tea candle burn down safely, as you tuck the crystal under your pillow and yourself into bed.

Negating Nightmares: Another Spell for Good Sleep

This spell can also be aided with herbal potions that help you sleep soundly (or just some unfussy chamomile tea), as nightmares are often caused by an agitated mind. If your nightmares come from a psychic interference or some deep well of anxiety or trauma, you may need to perform this spell fairly regularly for it to produce results. Casting it in conjunction with anxiety spells or other banishing spells can also increase its efficacy.

When to Perform: When necessary for peaceful sleep

How Long It Takes: About 10-15 minutes before bedtime

What You'll Need:

- ❖ 1 black taper candle
- ❖ 1 silver ribbon
- ❖ 1 silver coin

Steps:

- ❖ As with the previous spell, prepare your bedroom not only with cleansing or smudging but also with practical considerations (clean sheets, comfy blanket and pillow, soothing music, and so on).

- ❖ Tie your silver ribbon around your black candle: the silver symbolizes spiritual awakening and higher thinking, as it binds the banishing candle.

- ❖ Hold your coin in your left hand as you light your candle and cast your spell: *"These dreams that come before the dawn, make not me a frightened pawn. I ask the moon, so calm and sure to bring me peace just like a cure."*

- ❖ Let the candle burn for a few minutes, as you visualize a peaceful scene or a previous happy dream. Put the coin on your windowsill, snuff the black candle, and tie the ribbon around your wrist before bed. You can reuse these magical tools for three nights in a row, if necessary.

Chakra Spell Jar

Root Chakra Jar

To make this magic bottle to increase grounding and stability and heal your root chakra, you will need the following ingredients:

- ❖ A glass bottle with a stopper, any size
- ❖ Sea salt
- ❖ Hematite crystals
- ❖ Red carnelian crystals
- ❖ Bloodstone crystals
- ❖ Cedarwood oil
- ❖ Beetroot leaves
- ❖ Cayenne pepper
- ❖ White sage
- ❖ A red candle

Steps:

- ❖ Place the ingredients inside the bottle, leaving room for a little air. Cap the jar and drip some wax from the candle over the top to seal it.

- ❖ Meditate for ten minutes by picturing a red light spinning and glowing and breathing regularly. Hide the bottle in a secret place in your house.

Sacral Chakra Jar

To make this magic bottle to increase security and creativity and heal your sacral chakra, you will need the following ingredients:

- ❖ A glass bottle with a stopper, any size

- ❖ Sea salt

- ❖ Moonstone crystals

- ❖ Dark amber crystals

- ❖ Tigers eye crystals

- ❖ Sandalwood oil

- ❖ Orange peel

- ❖ Damiana powder

- ❖ An orange candle

Steps:

- ❖ Place the ingredients inside the bottle, leaving room for a little air. Cap the jar and drip a little wax of the candle over the top to seal it.

- ❖ Meditate for ten minutes by picturing an orange light glowing and pulsing following the rhythm of your breath. Hide the bottle in a secret place in your house.

Solar Plexus Chakra Jar

To make this magic bottle to boost your confidence and heal your solar plexus chakra, you will need the following ingredients:

- ❖ A glass bottle with a stopper, any size

- ❖ Sea salt

- ❖ Citrine crystals

- ❖ Light Agata crystals

- ❖ Calcite crystals

- ❖ Clove oil

- ❖ Lemongrass

- ❖ Ginger

- ❖ A yellow candle

Steps:

- ❖ Place the ingredients inside the bottle, leaving room for a little air. Cap the jar and drip some wax from the candle over the top to seal it.

- ❖ Meditate for ten minutes by picturing a yellow light glowing and pulsing following the rhythm of your breath. Hide the bottle in a secret place in your house.

Heart Chakra Jar

To make this magic bottle to give love to yourself and others and heal your heart chakra, you will need the following ingredients:

- A glass bottle with a stopper, any size
- Sea salt
- Jade crystals
- Rose quartz crystals
- Malachite crystals
- Lavender oil
- Jasmine
- Rose petals
- A green candle

Steps:

- Place the ingredients inside the bottle, leaving room for a little air. Cap the jar and drip some wax from the candle over the top to seal it.

- Meditate for ten minutes by picturing a shining green light glowing and beating while you inhale and exhale. Hide the bottle in a secret place in your house.

Throat Chakra Jar

To make this magic bottle to improve your communication, help you speak the truth, and heal your throat chakra, you will need the following ingredients:

- ❖ A glass bottle with a stopper, any size
- ❖ Sea salt
- ❖ Apatite crystals
- ❖ Turquoise crystals
- ❖ Aquamarine crystals
- ❖ Bergamot oil
- ❖ Sage
- ❖ Chamomile
- ❖ A blue candle

Steps:

- ❖ Place the ingredients inside the bottle, leaving room for a little air. Cap the jar and drip some wax from the candle over the top to seal it.

- ❖ Meditate for ten minutes by picturing a deep blue light glowing and moving to the rhythm of your breath. Hide the bottle in a secret place in your house.

Third Eye Chakra Jar

To make this magic bottle to improve your intuition, help you connect with the Universe, and heal your third eye chakra, you will need the following ingredients:

- ❖ A glass bottle with a stopper, any size
- ❖ Sea salt
- ❖ Azurite crystals
- ❖ Calcite crystals
- ❖ Sodalite crystals
- ❖ Mint oil
- ❖ Passionflower
- ❖ Sandalwood
- ❖ An indigo candle

Steps:

- ❖ Place the ingredients inside the bottle, leaving room for a little air. Cap the jar and drip some wax from the candle over the top to seal it.

- ❖ Meditate for ten minutes by picturing a gleaming indigo light glowing and beating while you breathe in and out. Hide the bottle in a secret place in your house.

Crown Chakra Jar

To make this magic bottle to improve your spiritual connections and heal your crown chakra, you will need the following ingredients:

- ❖ A glass bottle with a stopper, any size
- ❖ Sea salt
- ❖ Howlite crystals
- ❖ Sugilite crystals
- ❖ Alexandrite crystals
- ❖ Myrrh oil
- ❖ Lavander
- ❖ A violet candle

Steps:

- ❖ Place the ingredients inside the bottle, leaving room for a little air. Cap the jar and drip some wax from the candle over the top to seal it.

- ❖ Meditate for ten minutes by picturing a radiant violet light glowing and moving to the rhythm of your breath. Hide the bottle in a secret place in your house.

Spell for a Specific Person

Valentine's Day Spell Jar

Ingredients:

- ❖ Love oil
- ❖ Salt
- ❖ 1 jar with a lid
- ❖ Honey
- ❖ 1 candle (pink, red or white)
- ❖ Flower petals (optional)

How to Cast the Spell:

- ❖ Dress the candle with love oil. As you do this, think about bringing love to you as you put the oil on the candle and point it at yourself.

- ❖ To put the candle on your altar, you should put it in a candle holder.

- ❖ In the jar, put 5 drops of the oil in, and add 1 tablespoon of honey. To make the jar look pretty, you can put flower petals, such as roses, inside of it.

- ❖ Make sure the lid is on the jar and put it on your altar next to the candle.

- ❖ Sprinkle a little salt on your shrine. You can put salt around the candle and the jar to keep them safe. Any kind of salt you have in your kitchen will work. You can use it.

- ❖ As you light the candle, think about what you want to bring in. Think about the things that make this person unique (with or without thinking of any specific person). This is

Valentine's Day Love Spell Chant.

❖ Chant the chant over and over again like a mantra and then go into meditation; look down to find a love-themed meditative song to listen to while you clean your body in the bath.

❖ Burn it all the way through. If you need to leave the room, put it out and then start it again when you get back. Finish the candle next week.

Mother Moonlight

Ingredients:

- ❖ Full Moon night
- ❖ A place outside or a window facing the Moon

How to Cast the Spell:

- ❖ Outside, look at the moon. You can picture her energy coming to where you are and slowly bathing you.

- ❖ Think about the person you love for a while.

- ❖ Raise your arms and breathe in.

- ❖ Slowly put your hands on your lap to let the air out. One hand is on top of the other one.

- ❖ Make a noise: Full-Moon-Wiccan-Love-Spell

- ❖ Stay deep-breathed as you think about him (or her). Relax and meditate, letting the Moon's energy flow through you. Feel her strength and know that she will help you reach your goal.

- ❖ Once you feel strong, go back inside.

- ❖ Do this for three nights in a row.

Sugar Binding

Ingredients:

- ❖ Dish
- ❖ 1 lavender incense stick
- ❖ 1 red candle
- ❖ 1 teaspoon of sugar
- ❖ Red pen or marker
- ❖ Piece of paper

If you want to make a man fall in love with you, you should think of a specific person and be sure of your feelings.

Why this Spell Works

Sugar is an important ingredient in Kitchen Folk Magic because it helps to make people and things feel better. Make this Magic spell recipe to get the man you want safely and powerfully.

A simple chant and the power of a red candle will be all you need to try to make your heart's desires come true.

Sticky Kiss

Ingredients:

- ❖ 1 tablespoon of honey

- ❖ 1 red candle

- ❖ 1 piece of paper

This is a very easy and free love spell that you can cast right now with ingredients you can find in your kitchen. So, they're called "Kitchen Magic." What makes this spell "sweet" is the power of honey.

Why this Spell Works

A sweetening agent called honey can be used in Magic rituals. It can be used to make someone's mood or feelings more pleasant, which can make them closer to you. You can use the power of a red candle and honey to get what you want.

If you don't have any, a white candle or a pink candle can be used instead of red candles. Because the pink candle is so romantic but not so passionate, it will bring the person closest to you in a romantic but not too passionate way. Always put a white candle on your altar for extra protection. You can also make a circle.

Sugar Jar Love Spell

Ingredients:

- Jar

- Sugar

- Hibiscus, Rose, Lavender, Chamomile, Jasmine, Cinnamon, Orange, Lemon, Basil, Rosemary, Vanilla, and Oregano are some herbs and essential oils that you can use. You can choose any combination of them.

- Small piece of paper

- Red ink pen

- Rose quartz

- Pink or Red candle

How to Cast the Spell:

- Light a candle.

- What you write on your paper will depend on what you want:

- If you want to keep your relationship strong or attract a specific person, write your partner's name and birth date on paper. A circle is drawn around it.

- In the search for love, write down a few things you want your future partner to have.

- In the present tense, write your name and what you need to be proud of, or what you want for yourself.

- Using a few drops of wax from your candle, seal your paper into a scroll. You could also wrap the scroll with red or pink ribbon or thread if you'd rather. Add the scroll to the glass jar.

- Add your ingredients and the rose quartz to fill

209

the jar and cover the scroll.

- ❖ Take a small amount of the sugar mix and sprinkle it around your candle.

Seal your jar and hold it up to the flame while you say:

"Fire that flickers and burns bright.

Sweet dreams: I'll send you some tonight.

People are starting to fall in love with each other under this moon, which shines and glows. A heart is getting sweeter, and things are going to change soon.

Earth, Wind, Fire, and Sea: "This Is My Will, and So It Is!"
"

It's best to let the candle go out on its own (or extinguish it if planning to re-use it). Keep the jar next to your bed while you sleep.

Light a candle and repeat the spell once a week with a small pinch of your sugar mixture. Do this every week.

Honey Sweetening Jar Spell

Ingredients:

- ❖ Paper
- ❖ 1 pink candle
- ❖ Pen or pencil
- ❖ Honey (if you don't have honey, use sugar instead)
- ❖ 1 jar with a lid
- ❖ 1 of these herbs (fresh or dried): Bay leaf, Lavender, and Cinnamon.

How to Cast the Spell:

- ❖ The lid must be on the jar you use. It doesn't matter what kind of jar you use as long as it has a lid that seals well.
- ❖ Make sure to write the person's full name on the piece of paper that you're writing on.
- ❖ A pinch of the herb you want to use is all you need to do.

Sprinkle it on the paper. People who use Bay leaf, Lavender, and Cinnamon can get rid of and protect themselves.

- ❖ Fold the paper in half and put it in the jar.
- ❖ Pour some honey into the jar. Another spoonful should be added until the paper is fully covered. This spell is: Sweet Magic Spell
- ❖ Close the lid on the jar. Place the pink candle on the lid and then light it, as shown.
- ❖ When you think about the flame of the candle, imagine how the person will change their attitude toward you. In your mind, picture this person as someone who is kind, smiling, and

211

pays attention to you.

❖ Candles should never be left alone to burn. Keep the candle going once a week or whenever you want to. If you leave the room, put the candle out. Afterward, toss out any wax that is still left and keep the jar closed. It should be kept in a dark place where no one will touch it.

Full Moon Wish Spell

Ingredients:

- ❖ Pen
- ❖ 1 white candle
- ❖ Paper

How to Cast the Spell:

- ❖ Light the white candle and put it on a plate.

- ❖ Take a look at the flame and think about the element fire while you do this Think about how it can be life-giving, primal, passionate, and clean.

- ❖ Take three deep breaths.

- ❖ Say: The Full Moon Spell.

- ❖ Take a piece of paper and write down your request with a pen on it. To make your wish come true, let yourself go and write it down in as much detail as possible.

- ❖ Make sure the paper is under the dish. Keep it there until the candle is out. Candle safety: Don't leave the room if the candle is still going.

- ❖ You should blow out the candle when it is out. When you get the piece of paper, put it in your diary or witchy journal, or hide it in a secret place.

- ❖ Dispose of the body parts by burying them or putting them in the compost or trash.

'Far & Away' Jar

Ingredients:

- ❖ Paper
- ❖ 1 glass jar of any size (with a lid)
- ❖ Pen
- ❖ Coarse salt (sea salt or other)
- ❖ Vinegar (any kind: brown, white wine, red or cider)

How to Cast the Spell:

- ❖ To get rid of someone, write their full name on a small piece of paper.
- ❖ Imagine that the person is going to be gone for good. Fold the paper twice.
- ❖ When you're done, put the paper inside.
- ❖ Salt enough to cover the paper. A few tablespoons should be enough for you to get the right amount of food.
- ❖ Then, add 9 drops of vinegar and keep picturing how the person is gone from your life.
- ❖ In the jar, you can say: How to get rid of someone's spell
- ❖ You should close the jar and take it to a place far away from your home. You can bury it or throw it away in a trash can.

Herbal Harmony

Ingredients:

- ❖ 1 pink candle (or replace with a white candle)

- ❖ Water

- ❖ Chamomile tea (1 tea bag or 1 tablespoon of loose leaves)

How to Cast the Spell:

- ❖ Put on the kettle; you and your partner can light the candle while you wait for the water to boil. Take three deep breaths together.

- ❖ Empty your thoughts. Before any ritual, it's important to clear your mind and spirit, trying to let go of any bad thoughts. If you don't want to be completely silent, just be in the moment and enjoy each other.

- ❖ The tea should be added when the water has boiled. Then, pour the water. Pour theirs before yours. Let it cool down for 2 or 3 minutes before you eat it.

- ❖ chant this out loud: a spell with herbal tea to bring peace

- ❖ Taking the first sip of tea together, look at each other. Silence, candles, and good vibes are all around you right now. Enjoy them! Slowly drink your tea.

- ❖ Once you're done, pick up and wash the mugs and teapot with care. To be respectful, this should be done with a lot of care because it's also part of the ritual.

216

Chapter 6. How to Reverse a Spell

Spell Reversal

One of the best reasons for keeping your spellcasting personal as you first start learning is that it lessens the risk of consequences.

Because mistakes are bound to happen, you should start with simple spells that have only a few ingredients and a few steps involved.

As important as learning how to build a successful spell is, it's just as important for you to learn how to disassemble a spell. A spellcaster needs to know how to break down spells into separate components.

You may have heard that a spell is unbreakable. That's one of the biggest falsehoods about spellcasting. Sure, some spells are stronger than others. But even the strongest spells can be broken.

Reversing the Spell

To reverse a spell, simply cast the same spell but create an incantation to release the spell's control. Pour the liquid onto the base of the tree and repeat the incantation to release the spell. Pour a salt circle around the tree. Instead of writing a fresh spell, you can also recite the original spell in reverse. But like anything in magick, the more specific, the better!

You can now clean and wash the jar. Remember to cleanse and charge the jar so it's ready when you need it!

Conclusion

Conclusion

As you have already seen, the practice of witchcraft is not as scary, difficult, or even as evil as it's often portrayed. In fact, its origin came out of a good place of love, care, and responsibility. We all have this power within us, and you don't have to have special abilities to practice it. The only thing that is needed is the readiness and willingness to open your heart, mind, and spirit to its possibilities. As a beginner, the spells illustrated in the book are a fine way to start off your practice. The more you practice the better you get at the craft.

That way, you will build a strong foundation from which you will keep growing and building your skill as a witchcraft practitioner. Along the way, you will over and over again pause to think about new resources and visions. Ensure that you go slow and try to reflect a lot on what meaning these concepts personally bring to your life. It is also crucial to allow the freshly acquired ideas to be integrated into your own spirit. That is the only way that they can become "real' in your life as a practitioner of witchcraft. The spells and rituals will start being a part of who you are and will be in harmony with how you feel and think. One of the best ways to enhance your spiritual connection is with constant practice.

Never forget the witchcraft code of conduct that says;

"Mind the Threefold Law you should,

Three times bad and three times good''

This means that the moment you harm others with the practice, harm will come to you three times as much. Just like the law of karma. Therefore, whatever you practice, make sure that it does not bring harm to any individual.

You should always remember that learning the practice of witchcraft is a process that will never be complete. There will always be more information to acquire, more procedures to try out, and more knowledge to gain about your inner self. Just focus on taking it one step at a time, as each day unfolds and try to learn as much as you can. Consider your progress as a thrilling journey, and you will find yourself enjoying every single moment of it.

Printed in Great Britain
by Amazon

14381439R00132